# Inca Mythology

*Captivating Inca Myths of Gods, Goddesses, and Legendary Creatures*

© **Copyright 2019**

All Rights Reserved. No part of this book may be reproduced in any form without permission in writing from the author. Reviewers may quote brief passages in reviews.

Disclaimer: No part of this publication may be reproduced or transmitted in any form or by any means, mechanical or electronic, including photocopying or recording, or by any information storage and retrieval system, or transmitted by email without permission in writing from the publisher.

While all attempts have been made to verify the information provided in this publication, neither the author nor the publisher assumes any responsibility for errors, omissions or contrary interpretations of the subject matter herein.

This book is for entertainment purposes only. The views expressed are those of the author alone, and should not be taken as expert instruction or commands. The reader is responsible for his or her own actions.

Adherence to all applicable laws and regulations, including international, federal, state and local laws governing professional licensing, business practices, advertising and all other aspects of doing business in the US, Canada, UK or any other jurisdiction is the sole responsibility of the purchaser or reader.

Neither the author nor the publisher assumes any responsibility or liability whatsoever on the behalf of the purchaser or reader of these materials. Any perceived slight of any individual or organization is purely unintentional.

# Free Bonus from Captivating History (Available for a Limited time)

Hi History Lovers!

Now you have a chance to join our exclusive history list so you can get your first history ebook for free as well as discounts and a potential to get more history books for free! Simply visit the link below to join.

Captivatinghistory.com/ebook

Also, make sure to follow us on Facebook, Twitter and Youtube by searching for Captivating History.

# Contents

INTRODUCTION ................................................................ 1

**PART I: STORIES OF THE GODS** ................................... 4

    VIRACOCHA CREATES THE WORLD ............................................. 4

    THE TALE OF PACHACAMAC ...................................................... 9

    CONIRAYA AND THE MAIDEN .................................................. 13

    THE TALE OF HUATHACAURI ................................................... 19

    THE WANDERINGS OF PARIACACA ........................................... 27

    THE COMBAT OF PARIACACA AND HUALLALLO CARHUINCHO ..... 31

**PART II: INCA POLITICAL MYTHS** ............................ 35

    THE TALE OF MANCO CAPAC ................................................. 35

    THE TALE OF MAYTA CAPAC .................................................. 41

    TOPA INCA YUPANQUI AND MACAHUISA .................................. 44

    INCA HUAYNA CAPAC AND CONIRAYA ..................................... 47

## PART III: FIVE ANDEAN FOLKTALES AND AN INCA PLAY ........................................................................... 51

### THE MACAW WOMAN ................................................... 51
### THE CONDOR AND THE SHEPHERDESS ........................... 53
### THE MAIDEN AND THE THREE WARRIORS ..................... 58
### THE LLAMA-HERDER AND THE DAUGHTER OF THE SUN ............... 61
### THE LEGEND OF LAKE TITICACA .................................... 67
### THE TALE OF OLLANTAY .............................................. 69

## HERE'S ANOTHER BOOK THAT I THINK YOU'D BE INTERESTED IN: ....................................................... 83
## AND ANOTHER ONE… ............................................... 84
## BIBLIOGRAPHY ......................................................... 85

# Introduction

From its inception sometime in the thirteenth century to its fall after the arrival of the Spanish in the sixteenth, the Inca Empire was a complex and well-structured political and geographical unit that encompassed a great swath of western South America, from parts of what are now Ecuador and Colombia to the north to parts of Argentina and Chile to the south, while what is now Peru and parts of western Bolivia made up the central portion. The Inca Empire was not comprised of a single unitary culture but rather was a kind of federation of many peoples under the authority of the *Sapa Inca*, the emperor who ruled from the capital in Cuzco and who was said to be the son of the sun-god, Inti. The primary language of the empire was Quechua, but Aymara and other languages were also spoken by the diverse peoples who lived in the four *suyu*, or provinces, that made up the empire.

As with other Central and South American cultures that fell victim to Spanish colonialism, the myths of the Incas have been passed down to us through a Western, Christian filter, since many of these stories were collected by Spanish writers and written down with varying degrees of accuracy, completeness, and bias toward the indigenous cultures that produced them. We are further hampered with respect to Inca myth in that the pre-colonial Inca seem not to have had a written language, as did the Maya and Aztecs; therefore, we have no indigenous Inca texts that have survived colonial rapacity as we do with Mesoamerican cultures, and therefore we have nothing with which to compare the witnesses of Spanish writers. Further, texts that were compiled by indigenous Inca writers after the conquest betray the heavy influence of Christianization.

That said, it is important to note that the Incas did have a system of strings and knots, known as *quipu*, that they used to keep track of census data and goods, but there is considerable debate whether quipu might have been used to record narrative tales as well. Scholars such as Gary Urton have argued that some quipu that remain undeciphered might in fact contain such narratives. If these could be translated, they would be a valuable check on the testimony of early colonialist ethnographers.

Official Inca religion centered around the worship of the Sun in a temple complex in Cuzco, but Inti, the sun-god, was only one of many deities revered by the Incas. There were several creator-gods, who each had their own associated myths, but there were also hundreds of *huacas*, a kind of divine spirit being who could take on a corporeal form at will and which were venerated in shrines also known as *huacas* throughout the empire. Often these shrines centered on some kind of monument made of stone, and many such shrines and holy places remain standing throughout the Andean region today.

We see the importance of stone and the mountains, which are a primary geographical feature of the west coast of South America, throughout the tales presented in this book. Many of the stories contain a scene in which a divine or mortal figure is turned into stone, thus becoming a *huaca* that subsequently is revered as a holy site, while other tales contain a scene in which a figure is transformed into an entire mountain. The myths of the Inca gods in the first section of the book explain how the world was created and also detail the adventures of various deities as they vie for supremacy or act as tricksters in the worlds of mortals and *huacas* alike. The second section contains the origin myth of the Inca Empire, which was used to justify Inca political legitimacy. This section also presents other tales involving the mythologized deeds of Inca emperors and their interactions with divine beings. The final section contains a collection of Andean folktales and a prose narrative version of the eighteenth-century drama *Apu Ollantay*, which may have been based on an ancient Inca tale and which tells the story of the forbidden love between Cusi Coyllur, daughter of the Inca Pachacuti, and the brave warrior Ollantay, whose name also graces the Inca fortress of Ollantay-tambo just north of Cuzco.

Although this book presents these tales under the umbrella designation of "Inca myths," these are in fact stories from several diverse cultures. The gods who create and destroy, play tricks and journey through the world in human guise are regional beings, revered in particular places by particular peoples within the Inca world. What ties them all together is the human desire for reasons, for explanations of why the world is the way it is, and the desire to explore love, fear, loyalty, lust for power, and the many other things that make us human.

# PART I: STORIES OF THE GODS

## Viracocha Creates the World

*Some Inca origin myths center on the area around Lake Titicaca, which is located in the Andes mountain range on the border of southeastern Peru and central western Bolivia. Lake Titicaca is the largest lake in South America and is a striking feature of Andean geography that is easily visible from space. In Inca creation myths, Lake Titicaca and the Isla del Sol, the largest island within the lake, function as a kind of cosmic nexus from which the creator arises to make the world.*

*One of the primary creators in Inca mythology is a being called* Viracocha, *which can be translated as "foam of the sea." In his book on Inca myth, Gary Urton points out that Viracocha was primarily an Andean highland deity, and that in the lowlands, creation was thought to be the work of a being called* Pachacamac. *The highland myth states that Viracocha is the one who initiates creation, but when it is time to people the world, he draws on the aid of two sons, Imaymana Viracocha and Tocapu Viracocha. Each of the Viracochas goes in a different direction to call people into being and give them their cultures, languages, and instructions in how to live in the places they are to call home.*

*The fact that Viracocha apparently is some kind of trinity has led to speculation that the myth somehow became contaminated by Christian doctrine after Spain's conquest of Peru and the imposition of Catholic beliefs on the indigenous population. However, the concept of a triune god or of divine beings who otherwise work together in groups of three is found in many cultures throughout the world. Scholars therefore continue to debate whether the apparent threefold nature of Viracocha is a feature of native Inca belief or was something grafted onto the creation legend by the Incas in attempts to conform to the religious demands of their Christian conquerors.*

Long, long ago, there was darkness. And in the darkness was a lake. The skies were dark, and the waters of the lake were dark, and the name of the lake was Titicaca.

Out of the waters of the lake came Con Tici Viracocha Pachayachachic, the Creator of All Things. Viracocha arose from the depths of Lake Titicaca, from the darkness of the waters he arose, and around him he created a world. But it was a world without light, for Viracocha did not create either a sun or a moon, nor did he create any stars. And in this lightless world, Viracocha sculpted a race of giants, huge men and women to people the earth, and he painted them with all manner of colors.

"Live!" said Viracocha to the giants. "Live, and walk, and breathe, and talk. Live without quarrelling with one another. Live, and serve and obey your Creator!"

The giants came to life at Viracocha's word. They went about in the darkness of that world without sun or moon or stars. But soon they quarreled with one another, and they forgot to serve and obey Viracocha, so Viracocha turned some of them into great stones. Others he destroyed by opening up the earth beneath the giants' feet. The giants fell into the earth which closed over them. Yet others were destroyed by great waves that pulled them out to sea. None of the giants were ever seen again.

Viracocha was dismayed that his creation had failed. He made it rain for sixty days and sixty nights. It rained and rained, and soon the streams and rivers began to overflow their banks. The lakes overflowed their banks. The rain came down, and the water rose, and soon the whole world was covered by the waters of the flood. Everything Viracocha had made was washed away.

When the waters of the flood receded, Viracocha returned to Lake Titicaca. He went to the island that sits in the waters of the lake, the Island of the Sun. Viracocha thought that this time he would begin his creation differently. This time, Viracocha created lights in the heavens before making anything else. He created the sun, the moon, and the stars, and he put them in their places in the heavens.

The sun rose, and it was pleased with its brightness. "I am the brightest thing in the heavens," said the sun. "Everyone will look at me in wonder."

Then the moon rose, and it was even brighter than the sun. This made the sun jealous. The sun reached down and took up a handful of ashes. It threw the ashes at the moon. The moon's face became mottled with the ashes that the sun threw at it, dimming its light.

After creating the lights in the heavens, Viracocha left the Island of the Sun and went to Tiahuanaco. Viracocha took stones that he found on the banks of the lake. He molded the stones into the likeness of people, but he did not make these new people into giants. He gave the different people different features. He gave them different clothes to wear. He gave them languages to speak and songs to sing, and he gave them seeds so that they might grow their own food.

When the people had all been made, Viracocha brought them to life. Then he sent them on a journey below the earth. The people journeyed below the earth, each turning to the way that they must go, according to the dress they wore and the language they spoke. They came up out of the earth when they arrived at the places that Viracocha had given them to live. Some of them came out of the waters of rivers and springs. Some of them came out of the mouths of caves. Some of them came out of the stone of the mountains. Wherever the people emerged, there they made their homes.

Con Tici Viracocha had two sons. One was called Imaymana Viracocha. The other was called Tocapu Viracocha. Before sending the people on their journeys below the earth, Con Tici Viracocha showed them to his sons. Con Tici Viracocha said, "Look at the people carefully. Remember how they look and how they dress. Remember how they speak, and remember the songs they sing. For we will have duties to the peoples of the earth once they have emerged into the places that will be their homes."

Con Tici Viracocha sent Imaymana up into the mountains and down into the jungle. Tocapu Viracocha went to the place where the sea meets the land and went along the coastline. Con Tici Viracocha went along the river valley toward Cuzco. In all those places, each Viracocha proclaimed loudly to all the peoples that they were to obey Con Tici Viracocha Pachayachachic, who commanded that they make their homes in the places they had emerged and that they multiply and people the earth. And it was then that the people came forth from the springs and rivers, from the caves and mountains. They came forth at the command of Con Tici Viracocha, the command that was spoken by his sons and by Con Tici Viracocha himself. As they called to the people to come forth into their new lands, Viracocha and his sons taught the people all the things they needed to know to live. They showed the people how to grow plants for food. They showed the people which plants could be used for medicine. They taught the people the names of all the plants and creatures.

Viracocha then decided to make a journey. He put on his traveling cloak and took up his staff and set off down the road. Northwards Viracocha walked, going toward the city of Cuzco. On his way, he arrived at a town called Cacha. Now, the people who emerged in this place at the call of Viracocha and his sons were called the Cana people. They came into the world armed for war, and they were very fierce and dangerous people. The Cana saw Viracocha coming along the road, but they did not recognize their Creator. They armed themselves and went forth from their village, thinking that they would kill this stranger who dared to come near their lands.

Viracocha saw the armed men coming toward him. He knew that they did not mean him well, and he was angry that they would attack the one who had made them and given them a good place in which to live. Viracocha raised his hands to the heavens and called down a rain of fire. The fire landed on the hillside where the armed men were, setting the grass alight. The Cana people then realized their mistake. They fell down before Viracocha and begged his forgiveness. Viracocha took pity on them. He took his staff and put out all the flames, but he did not cause the grass to regrow. That place remained burnt and dry ever after, and even the stones themselves were altered by the flames of Viracocha: the fire burned away their heaviness so that even the largest of stones could be carried by one man alone.

Leaving the Cana people behind, Viracocha continued walking northwards. Ever northwards he walked until he came to a place called Urcos, where he climbed up the mountain and sat down upon its peak. There he called forth another group of people, that they might live upon the heights of the mountain. He called them forth, and they came, and he explained to him that he was the Creator who had made them. The people worshipped Viracocha. They made a *huaca*, which is a place sacred to the gods, and there they placed an image of Viracocha that was all made out of gold, and they set it upon a bench that was also made out of gold.

When the people of Urcos were well established in their new home, and when the *huaca* had been constructed and properly consecrated, Viracocha resumed his journey northwards. He went along the road to Cuzco, and as he went, he called forth new peoples and instructed them in the ways they were to live. Finally, he arrived at Cuzco, which is the name that Viracocha himself gave to that place. Viracocha called into being a man named Alcaviza, who was made the first lord of Cuzco. Then Viracocha made a command that the Inca people emerge in that place once Viracocha had left to continue his journey.

On and on Viracocha journeyed, going along the road until he came to the place that is now called Puerto Viejo. In Puerto Viejo, the sons of Viracocha came to meet their father. Once they had all gathered, Viracocha and his sons went down to the coast, for that is where they departed from this world. A great crowd of people had gathered to greet their Creator and hear what he had to say to them. Viracocha said, "I must leave you now, but I will tell you of things that are to come. In time, people will arrive in your lands, people who claim to be myself, to be Viracocha the Creator of All Things. You must not listen to them, for they speak falsehood. I alone am Con Tici Viracocha, and I will care for you by sending messengers who will protect you and teach you things I wish you to learn."

After Viracocha spoke to the people, he and his sons walked out onto the ocean. They walked ever westwards until they passed out of sight, and the people marveled to see them walking on the water which they trod as lightly as they had done the solid ground. Thus it is that the people call their Creator Viracocha, which means "foam of the sea."

And that is the tale of how Viracocha created the world and filled it with people.

## The Tale of Pachacamac

*Whereas Viracocha was a creator-god for the highland Inca, Pachacamac was worshiped by lowland coastal peoples. Unfortunately, most of the mythology pertaining to Pachacamac has been lost, partly because his cult was displaced by sun worship when the Incas took over the area that had worshiped Pachacamac and partly as a result of the Christianization of Peru after the conquest. Gary Urton notes that the main myth about Pachacamac was preserved by Antonio de la Calancha, a Spanish cleric who wrote a chronicle of the Incas in the middle of the seventeenth century.*

*Pachacamac is also the name of an important archaeological site that contains the ruins of several temples and other buildings. One of these was the only temple to Pachacamac in the whole of the Inca Empire, and as such, it became a site for pilgrimage. The temple was sacked and looted by the conquistador Hernando Pizarro in 1533.*

Long, long ago, in the very beginning of things, there was a son of the Sun, and his name was Con. Con had great power: if he came to a mountain that was too high for him to climb, he would lower it, and if he came to a valley that was too low for him to cross, he would raise it. Con strode about the world creating people to live in it. He created the people, and he also created everything they needed for food. He gave them good land to till, land that was fertile and easily worked, and plenty of rain to water their crops and orchards.

But all was not well with the people. They behaved very badly and did not treat Con with reverence. Con therefore decided he would punish the people. This he did by causing the rain to cease falling. All the fields that the people used to grow their food dried up and became like deserts, and the only water they had came from the rivers and streams that flowed through their lands. The people then had to work many times harder to grow their food because they no longer had enough rain from the sky. They had to dig channels from the rivers to bring water into their fields. It was very hard work, and the crops did not grow as well as they did before Con's punishment.

Con was not the only child of the Sun. A brother he had, child of the Sun and the Moon, named Pachacamac. Pachacamac saw all the people that his brother created, and he thought to himself that if he were the creator, he could do much better. So Pachacamac drove Con out of the world. He then changed all the people Con had created into beasts. Some of them became monkeys. Some became foxes. Some became birds. But when Pachacamac was done, there were no more people to live in the land and to terrace and till the soil.

Pachacamac then created a man and a woman. But he did not provide food for them, and soon the man died. The woman did not know what to do. She was all alone in the world, and she had nothing to eat. She faced the Sun and said, "O Father Sun, I have nothing to eat. I have no family. I do not know what to do. Please help me!"

The Sun looked down upon the woman and saw that she was very beautiful. The Sun desired her, and so he sent his rays down upon her to get her with child. The child grew in the woman's womb and was born after only four days.

Pachacamac saw that the woman had borne a child by the Sun. This made him very angry and jealous. Pachacamac swore revenge, and so he took away the child and tore him into pieces. Pachacamac then scattered the pieces all around the land, and from the pieces, plants useful for food began to spring up. From the teeth sprang maize. From the bones sprang manioc. From the flesh sprang all manner of other fruits and vegetables.

The Sun saw what Pachacamac had done with his child and sorrowed greatly. He decided to make for himself another son, using the parts of the body that Pachacamac had not scattered. The Sun took the penis and the navel of the dismembered child, and from these pieces created another whole boy, whom he named Vichama. Just as the Sun likes to travel across the sky, so Vichama was seized by a desire to travel, and so one day, he set forth, leaving his mother behind.

When Pachacamac found out that the Sun had made another child from the pieces of the first one, he fell into a rage. He went to where the woman was, and he killed her. Then he took her body and gave it to the vultures and condors for their food. Then Pachacamac made a new man and a new woman, and they had many children, and their children had many children, and finally the land was peopled again. Pachacamac decided that the people needed a way to govern themselves, and so he named some of them to be *curacas*, who had authority over all the others.

After a time, Vichama returned from his journey. He wept to hear that Pachacamac had slain his mother and thrown her body to the vultures and condors to eat. Vichama went out and looked for all the pieces of his mother's body. He carefully put them back together, and when he was done, she was a whole woman again. Then Vichama brought her back to life.

Pachacamac saw that Vichama had come back and that he had brought his mother back to life. He feared Vichama's power and his anger. Pachacamac therefore went down to the seashore where he went out into the waves, going farther and farther until the water swallowed him up and he was lost from sight.

Once Pachacamac was gone, Vichama turned all the people Pachacamac had created into stone. But the ones who had been curacas when they were alive, he turned into *huacas* to be used as shrines for honoring the gods. Thus it was that the curacas kept the high status that Pachacamac had given them.

Yet again was the world unpeopled. Vichama therefore prayed to his father, the Sun, to help him make more people to live on the earth. The Sun gave Vichama three eggs. One egg was made of gold. One was of silver. The third was of copper. One by one, Vichama opened the eggs, and from them sprang different kinds of people. From the golden egg sprang the curacas and the nobles. From the silver egg sprang women. From the copper egg sprang commoners, both men and women, and their children. And in this way, the world was filled with people once again.

# Coniraya and the Maiden

*In this tale, we see Viracocha going by the name Coniraya in his guise as a trickster, and we also see how very human Inca deities could be, feeling lust and pride, shame and delight. This legend also functions as a just-so story, explaining how certain animals came to have their distinctive traits, for example, why the condor feasts on dead llamas and why the skunk smells so bad.*

*The Incas, like many other cultures around the world, also told stories of mysterious, miraculous births. In this case, the woman Cavillaca becomes pregnant when she eats an enchanted fruit of the lucuma tree, which is an evergreen that grows in the Andean valleys in Peru and Ecuador.*

One day, in the beginning of the world, Coniraya Viracocha had a mind to go on a journey. He had finished creating the land and the plants and the animals, the birds were in the sky, and the people were living in the places he had given them for their homes. His work of creation was done, and so Coniraya felt it was time to journey about the world.

Coniraya took up his staff and gave himself the appearance of a very old, very poor man. His skin was wrinkled, and his hair was white. He leaned upon his staff as though he needed its support. And in this guise, Coniraya set out upon the road. He went to many places, and everywhere he went, the people there treated him ill. "Go away, old man!" they would shout at him. "We have no use for an old beggar such as yourself!"

But Coniraya paid them no mind. He continued on his way, seeing what there was to be seen.

One day, Coniraya came upon a maiden who was sitting beneath a lucuma tree. The maiden was named Cavillaca, and she was a *huaca*, or divine spirit being. Cavillaca was busy at her weaving, and her clever fingers pulled at the threads on her loom, turning the bright wool into something beautiful.

Now, Cavillaca was very beautiful, and all the male *huacas* vied for her favor, but she never paid any mind to their advances, remaining unwed and unknown by any man. Coniraya saw Cavillaca and desired her for himself, but well he knew that she would not have him, so he thought to have a child by her by means of a trick. Coniraya transformed himself into a bird and lit on a branch of the lucuma tree. There he took some of his seed and turned it into a ripe lucuma fruit. He dropped the fruit near the woman and waited to see what she would do. Cavillaca noticed the bright fruit on the ground next to her. She had not eaten for some time and was hungry, so she picked up the fruit and ate it. And in this way Cavillaca became with child without ever having relations with a man.

When her nine months were done, Cavillaca gave birth to a beautiful child. She nursed the child at her breast and wondered often who the father could be. The child grew, happy and strong, and soon was able to crawl about. It was then that Cavillaca decided to find out who the father of her child was. She sent a message to all the other *huacas*, saying, "I wish to know who the father of my child is. If you know him, come and tell me." She told them that she would meet with them on a certain day in a place called Anchi Cocha.

All the *huacas* were overjoyed to hear Cavillaca's summons. They hoped that she would choose one of them for a husband at the meeting. On the day of the meeting, they dressed in their very best finery and took their seats in the place Cavillaca had set aside. Cavillaca showed her child to them and said, "Here is my child. I wish to know who the father is. Do any of you know him? Which of you is the father?"

But all the men sat silently, for none could truthfully claim to be the father of the child.

Now, Coniraya Viracocha also had heard Cavillaca's summons, and he was there at the meeting. He sat at the edge of the group, wearing his beggar's rags and leaning on his staff, his old man's white beard trailing down toward his chest. But even though he knew himself to be the father of the child, he did not speak out, and Cavillaca did not address him, thinking a poor beggar not worthy of her notice.

When none of the fine young men admitted to being the father of the child, Cavillaca said, "If you will not claim the child as your own, the child shall claim his own father. I shall set him down on the ground, and the one to whom he goes must be his father." Then she set the child on the ground and said, "Go and find the one who begot you!"

The child crawled through the crowd of young men, not stopping to greet any of them. He kept going, crawling on all fours as infants do, until he came to Coniraya. There the infant stopped and pulled himself up onto his father's knee.

Cavillaca saw who the infant had greeted and was dismayed. "Alas!" she cried. "Alas that the father of my child is a lowly beggar, a poor man of no account!"

Weeping, Cavillaca snatched up her child and ran from that place, going straight down to the shore where she thought to cast herself and her child into the sea. She ran across the sand and out into the waves and did not stop until she came to the deep water, where she and her child were turned to stone. And to this day, there are two stones in that place that look like people.

When Cavillaca ran away, Coniraya followed her. He ran after her as fast as he could, calling out her name, but she soon was so far ahead of him he did not know which way she had gone. As Coniraya tried to follow Cavillaca, he came upon a condor.

"Brother Condor," said Coniraya, "tell me, did you see a young woman run past here?"

"Yes, I did," said the condor. "She went that way. You should find her soon."

"I am grateful to you," said Coniraya, "and so I shall give you a gift. I will give you a long life. I will let you eat your fill of any dead animals you shall find upon the mountains. And people who kill you will also die."

Coniraya left the condor and returned to his search for Cavillaca. Soon Coniraya came upon a skunk.

"Sister Skunk," he said, "tell me, did you see a young woman run past here?"

"Yes, I did," said the skunk. "She went that way. But I doubt one as old as yourself could catch her; she ran like the wind."

Coniraya felt insulted by what the skunk said to him, so he laid a curse upon her. "Never shall you see daylight! You will go about only at night, and you will smell so bad that no other animals will want to come near you!"

Coniraya left the skunk and returned to his search for Cavillaca. Soon Coniraya came upon a puma.

"Brother Puma," said Coniraya, "tell me, did you see a young woman run past here?"

"Yes, I did," said the puma. "She went that way not long ago. You should find her soon."

"I am grateful to you," said Coniraya, "and so I shall give you a gift. You shall eat many fat llamas, and if people kill you, they will do it so that they can wear your head at festivals. That way you will always get to dance at festivals, too."

Coniraya left the puma and returned to his search for Cavillaca. Soon Coniraya met up with a fox.

"Brother Fox," said Coniraya, "tell me, did you see a young woman run past here?"

"Yes, I did," said the fox, "but that was some time ago. She must be very far from here by now. I don't think you'll ever catch up to her."

What the fox said made Coniraya very angry indeed. "A curse upon you!" said Coniraya. "You will always slink about craftily, and people will say of you that you are a thief and a trickster. If they kill you, they won't even use your body for food, and they won't even use your pelt for clothing or ornament!"

In the same way as he had met the other animals, Coniraya came upon a falcon.

"Sister Falcon," said Coniraya, "have you seen a young maiden running past here?"

"I have indeed," said the falcon, "and not very long ago. I think you must be close behind her."

"A blessing upon you," said Coniraya. "You shall have other birds for your food in great plenty. Sometimes people will kill you, but when they do, they will honor you with the sacrifice of a llama. They will put you on their heads when they dance at festivals. That way you will always get to dance at festivals, too."

Coniraya went upon his way, still chasing after Cavillaca. He ran and he ran until he came across some parakeets. He asked them the same question he had asked the other animals, and they replied, "Oh, she is far away from here. She was running so very swiftly, you'll never catch up with her no matter how hard you try."

"A curse upon you!" said Coniraya. "You will ever fly about screeching and screaming, and people will hate you and chase you away from their fields and orchards."

Everywhere Coniraya went, he asked for news of the maiden Cavillaca. If he was given good news and encouragement, he gave a blessing. But those who gave him bad news, he cursed.

On and on Coniraya ran, chasing after Cavillaca. But he never caught her. Coniraya came to the seashore and found that the maiden and her infant had gone out into the deep ocean where they had been turned to stone.

Seeing that there was no point in trying to find Cavillaca any more, Coniraya turned back inland. He walked until he came to the place where the daughters of Pachacamac lived, along with a giant snake who was their guardian. The mother of the girls was named Urpay Huachac, and when Coniraya arrived at that place, he found the mother was away, for she had gone to visit Cavillaca in her new home in the sea.

Coniraya looked upon Pachacamac's daughters, and he desired them greatly. He went into the house and made love to the eldest daughter, but when he tried to do the same with the younger one, she turned herself into a dove and flew away. And so it was that their mother was called Urpay Huachac, which means "Gives Birth to Doves."

Now, at that time, all the fish that there were in the world lived in a little pond near Urpay Huachac's house. Not a single fish was in the ocean. Coniraya was angry that the younger daughter would not sleep with him, so he took all the fish out of the pond and cast them into the ocean, saying, "Urpay Huachac has gone into the ocean to visit Cavillaca. Why don't you go and join them there!" And that is how the ocean came to be filled with fish.

After throwing all the fish into the ocean, Coniraya went away from that place and continued his journey. But soon Urpay Huachac returned home, and her daughters told her all that Coniraya had done while he was there. Urpay Huachac was furious that Coniraya dared to sleep with her eldest daughter and that he dared to go after the younger one as well, so Urpay Huachac went running after Coniraya as fast as she could go, calling his name all the while.

Soon enough, Coniraya heard Urpay Huachac calling for him, and so he stopped to wait for her. "What do you want of me?" he said.

"I wish to remove the lice from your head," said Urpay Huachac.

"Very well," said Coniraya, and he let her pick the lice from his head.

But Urpay Huachac had a plan. She intended to destroy Coniraya in revenge for what he had done to her daughters. Some say that Urpay Huachac made a great hole open up in the ground so that she could throw Coniraya into it. Some say that she created a great stone that she intended to drop onto his head. But whatever plan she had, Coniraya knew that Urpay Huachac did not mean him well, so he left her, saying that he needed to relieve himself. Once he was out of her sight, he ran off to another village, and thus he escaped Urpay Huachac's wrath.

And so it was that Coniraya went on his journey about the world, seeing what there was to be seen and playing tricks on people and *huacas* alike.

## The Tale of Huathacauri

*One of the features of Inca mythology is the concept of multi-partite gods. We see this with Viracocha, who seems to have been conceived as a trinity, and also with Pariacaca, a god who apparently is five beings in one. Not only is Pariacaca a complex being, but apparently, he is able to engender a son even before he himself is born: the hero of this tale, Huathacauri, is the son of Pariacaca, but Pariacaca himself is still confined within the five condor eggs of his own genesis.*

*Although he is the son of a god, Huathacauri is a poor man. He falls in love with a rich man's daughter and manages to marry her, but in doing so, he falls afoul of his wealthy, prideful brother-in-law, whom Huathacauri bests in a series of contests and who is eventually transformed into a deer. This myth therefore also functions as a cautionary tale against both pride and the mistreatment of the less fortunate.*

*This story and others about the god Pariacaca are recorded in the so-called Huarochirí Manuscript. It is written in Quechua and was compiled in the sixteenth century by Francisco de Avila, a Spanish cleric whose mission was to eradicate traditional Inca beliefs and replace them with Christianity. This manuscript, which was rediscovered in a Madrid library in 1939, was partially destroyed during World War II, although various modern copies of its contents survive. The manuscript is devoted to myths, legends, and religious beliefs from the Huarochirí province, which is an area in west-central Peru in the vicinity of Lima.*

Once there was a man named Huathacauri who was so poor that he lived on potatoes he gleaned from others' fields that he then roasted in pits on the hillside. Poor he may have been, but Huathacauri was the son of the mighty god Pariacaca, and so his life was blessed, and he performed many marvels.

Not far away from where the poor man lived there was a very rich man named Tamta Ñamca. Tamta Ñamca lived in a house thatched with the colorful feathers of birds, and the soft, thick thatch gleamed in the sun so that it could be seen from very far away. Tamta Ñamca also owned a vast herd of llamas, but what was astonishing was not their numbers but rather their colors. Just as birds have feathers of red, blue, and green, so too did Tamta Ñamca's llamas have hair of red, blue, and green, so that when they were shorn there was no need to dye the wool before spinning it into fine thread, and the wool from Tamta Ñamca's llamas made the best thread in the whole world.

People from all around that place saw how splendid Tamta Ñamca's house was and how large and colorful his llama herd was, and they said to one another, "Tamta Ñamca is a fine fellow! See how wealthy he is? Surely he must be kin to a divine being, or perhaps he is divine himself! Come, let us go and ask him for advice, for he must know a great many things."

Except Tamta Ñamca wasn't really all that wise, nor was he divine at all, but he was flattered by what the people said about him, and so he pretended to know a great many things that he did not know. So clever and deceitful was Tamta Ñamca that he managed to convince the people of his wisdom, and after hearing them sing his praises continually, he began to think to himself, "Perhaps what the people say about me is true. Perhaps I really am a god!"

This went on for some time until one day Tamta Ñamca became very sick indeed, and despite the efforts of all the best doctors, no one could find a cure for his ailment. Years went by, and still Tamta Ñamca was very ill, so the people began to wonder how wise he really was if he could not find a cure for his own sickness. They also began to wonder whether maybe they had been fooled by him, and so they began to turn against him.

One day, after Tamta Ñamca had been on his sickbed for many years, Huathacauri was sleeping on a mountainside near the rich man's home. In the night, Huathacauri was wakened by voices. Not knowing who was speaking and fearing robbers who might do him harm, Huathacauri held very still and listened. Soon he discerned that the voices were not those of men but rather of two foxes who had met in their prowls that night and were exchanging news of the places they had been.

"Let me tell you what I heard in Upper Villca," said one fox to the other. "You know that rich lord who lives in Anchi Cocha, the one whose house is all roofed with feathers and who claims to be a god?"

"I do indeed," said the second fox. "Have you news of him?"

"Yes," said the first fox. "He has been very ill for many years, and nobody knows what is wrong or how to cure him. But I know the cause, and I know how it might be cured.

"That rich man is ill because one day his wife was toasting maize for another man who had come to visit, and one of the kernels of maize popped out of the pan and fell into her lap. She picked up the kernel and put it on the plate with the others, and the man ate it, which is just the same as if he had slept with her. As a punishment, two serpents have come to roost in the rafters of their home, and a two-headed toad has burrowed its way under their grinding stone, and it is these loathsome things that are causing the rich man's illness."

"That is quite a tale!" said the second fox. "It is too bad for that man and his family; no one will ever happen upon that cure by themselves. His younger daughter will spend the rest of her days tending her father instead of marrying well like her older sister did."

The two foxes talked of many other things before bidding each other good night and going home to their kits, but Huathacauri did not listen to much of it. His mind was full of the plight of the rich man and how he might use this knowledge to his own advantage. Huathacauri also thought about what the foxes had said about the rich man's daughters.

In the morning, Huathacauri went down into the town where Tamta Ñamca lived and began asking after the health of the rich man. One of the people he asked was Tamta Ñamca's younger daughter. "My father is the one who is ill," said the maiden.

"Oh, that is very sad indeed," said Huathacauri.

"Yes," she replied, "for no one has been able to cure him for many years, and he suffers greatly."

"Take me to see your father," said Huathacauri. "Perhaps I can help him."

Together the young people went to Tamta Ñamca's house, where the rich man lay in bed surrounded by doctors who murmured to each other about what a sad case it was and sometimes argued about what cure they should try next.

The daughter, whose name was Chaupi Ñamca, brought Huathacauri to her father's bedside and told him that the young man thought he could cure his illness. When the doctors heard this, they all started laughing. "What is a young beggar like you going to do that none of us wise and learned men haven't already tried? Be off with you!"

But Tanta Ñamca said, "Let him come to me and say what he wants to do. None of you has been able to cure me, so I may as well listen to what this young man wants to try. I don't care that he's poor and dressed in rags as long as he can make me well again."

Huathacauri went to Tanta Ñamca's bedside and said, "Sir, I do think I can cure you, but I will do so only on one condition: you must give me your youngest daughter to be my bride."

"With a good will I shall do this if you can make me well again," said Tanta Ñamca.

Huathacauri explained that Tanta Ñamca's illness was caused by the serpents in the rafters and the two-headed toad beneath the grinding stone, and that they had come to make Tanta Ñamca sick after his wife gave the grain of maize that had fallen into her lap to another man.

"If I get rid of the serpents and the toad, you will get well," said Huathacauri. "And when you have gotten well, you must stop thinking yourself a god, for a god would not let himself get sick. Instead, you must worship my father, Pariacaca, who will come into the world in just a few days."

Tanta Ñamca gladly agreed to all this, so Huathacauri set about hunting the vile animals that were making the rich man ill. First, he went up into the rafters of the house and killed the serpents. Then he went out to where the grinding stone was and lifted it up. When the two-headed toad saw Huathacauri, it ran away into a nearby ravine and made its home in a spring there. And this is why when people go to that spring, they go mad.

Once the vermin had been killed or driven away, Tanta Ñamca became well again. He kept his promise to Huathacauri, and soon his daughter and the poor man became man and wife.

Now, Huathacauri's wife had a sister who was married to a rich and powerful man. This man was ashamed that his sister-in-law had married a wandering beggar, and he vowed to get his revenge. The brother-in-law went to Huathacauri and said, "We should see who of us is the better man. I propose we have a drinking and dancing contest."

Huathacauri accepted his brother-in-law's challenge, and then he went up the mountainside where there were five eggs. In the eggs was Pariacaca, Huathacauri's father. He was still inside the eggs, for the time had not yet come for him to come into the world. Huathacauri went to the eggs and told his father that he had been challenged to a drinking and dancing contest. He asked what advice Pariacaca might have for him.

"Go to that mountain over there and pretend to be a dead guanaco," said Pariacaca from inside the eggs. "I'm expecting a fox and a skunk to visit me tomorrow morning. They usually bring a jar full of maize beer with them. The skunk brings a drum, and the fox also brings his panpipes, but when they see you, they'll set those down and go over to you to start to eat you. When they do that, jump up in the form of a man and scream as loudly as you can. They'll be so frightened that they'll run away and forget their jar and their pipes and their drum. Then you can come here and get those things and take them down to the village to use for the contest."

Huathacauri did as Pariacaca said, and when he had frightened away the skunk and the fox, he picked up their belongings and went down to the village to have the contest with his brother-in-law. The brother-in-law went first in the dance. He danced with all his wives, and he had hundreds of them. Then it was Huathacauri's turn. He danced with only his one wife, but he played the skunk's drum as he danced, and every time he struck the drum, the earth shook. The people declared that Huathacauri had won the dancing contest because while the rich man had many wives to dance with him, the whole earth had danced with Huathacauri.

Then it was time for the drinking contest. The people served cup after cup after cup of maize beer to Huathacauri, but no matter how much he drank, he never became drunk. When it was Huathacauri's turn to serve, he picked up the jar of beer he had taken from the fox and the skunk and went around serving all the people. No matter how much beer he poured out, there was always more in the jar, and when the people drank their cups of beer, they each fell down drunk after only one sip. And so Huathacauri also won the drinking contest.

The brother-in-law was enraged that Huathacauri had beaten him so easily in the drinking and dancing contests, so he proposed another challenge. "Let's dance in the plaza wearing our best puma skins," he said. "Whoever is best adorned and dances best will be the winner."

Now, the brother-in-law was a very rich man, and he had many fine puma skins. He thought that it would be easy to win this contest because there was no way a poor beggar such as Huathacauri would have even one raggedy puma skin, never mind the fine collection that the rich man had.

Huathacauri was undaunted. He went up the mountain where the eggs were and asked his father what to do about this contest.

"Do you see that mountain over there?" said Pariacaca from inside the eggs. "On the side of that mountain is a fountain, and next to the fountain is a fine puma skin. Go there and take the skin. You can wear that for your contest."

Huathacauri did as Pariacaca instructed. Near the fountain he found a fine red puma skin which he put on. Huathacauri returned to the village and announced that he was ready for the challenge. The rich man was astonished that Huathacauri was wearing such a fine puma skin, but he thought to himself that surely the poor beggar would never be able to dance as well as a rich man. And so, the brother-in-law did his dance in his puma skin, and the people thought that he had danced very well indeed and looked very fine in his puma skin. But when Huathacauri danced, a rainbow appeared in the sky above his head, and so the people judged that Huathacauri had won the contest.

The rich man was ashamed and angry that Huathacauri had beaten him yet again, so he proposed a fourth contest. "Let us see who can build a house the quickest," he said.

Huathacauri agreed to the contest, and so the rich man began right away to build the house. The rich man hired many workers to come and build the house for him, but Huathacauri merely saw to the foundations of his and then spent the rest of the day with his wife. At the end of the day, the rich man's house was nearly finished, but Huathacauri's was still only the foundations. But that night, birds, serpents, and many other kinds of animals came to Huathacauri's house and put up the walls for him.

In the morning, Huathacauri's brother-in-law was astonished to see that the poor man's house was nearly finished, just as his own was. So, he proposed that the next challenge would be to see who could build the best roof. Guanacos and vicuñas brought the thatch for Huathacauri's house, and soon the roof was finished. The other man waited for his thatch to be brought on llamas, but it never arrived because a bobcat who was friends with Huathacauri charged the llamas and drove them over a cliff. And so Huathacauri won that contest, too.

Then Huathacauri said to his brother-in-law, "We have had many contests, but you have always been the one to propose them. If I propose a challenge, will you accept?"

"Yes, I will accept your challenge," said the rich man, thinking that he would finally have a chance to defeat Huathacauri.

"Let's put on blue tunics and white breechcloths and dance," said Huathacauri. "Whoever dances best will be the winner."

"Agreed," said the rich man, and so they put on their blue tunics and white breechcloths and went into the plaza to dance.

The rich man danced first, but as he was dancing, Huathacauri ran at him, screaming as fiercely as he possibly could. The rich man was so frightened by Huathacauri that he turned into a deer and bounded away out of the village and up the mountainside. When the rich man's wife saw that her husband had fled in the form of a deer, she went running after him.

"Run all you like!" shouted Huathacauri. "I'm tired of all your contests! I'm tired of you thinking that you're the best just because you are wealthy! You thought you would have revenge on me for being poor? No, it is I who shall have revenge on you!"

So Huathacauri went running after them, and soon he caught up with the wife. He grabbed her and stood her upside down on her head, where she turned into stone. And to this day, in that place is a stone that looks like the lower half of a woman's body, sticking out of the ground as if she were upside down. But the rich man ran away into the mountains in the form of a deer and was never seen or heard from again.

And these are all the deeds that Huathacauri did in the time before Pariacaca emerged from the five eggs.

## The Wanderings of Pariacaca

*Pariacaca, a primary god of the Huarochirí region, is a water deity that is five beings in one. We see his association with water here when he calls down rain that brings about a mudslide upon people who have disrespected him and also in his work to create canals for irrigation of crops in an area that is experiencing drought. Like many other deities found in myths the world over, Pariacaca also is susceptible to the charms of beautiful women, and here he falls for a female huaca named Chuqui Suso.*

When Pariacaca decided to come into the world, he first appeared as a clutch of five condor eggs on the side of a mountain. There he waited until the time was right, and then the eggs hatched into five fine condors. The condors flew out over the mountains, but eventually they turned into men who journeyed throughout the world.

One day, Pariacaca went to a Yunca village. The villagers were celebrating a feast that day. They were rejoicing and eating much food and getting very drunk on maize beer. Pariacaca went to join them, sitting at the very end of the feast in the lowest place, as is fitting for a visiting stranger. He waited and waited, but no one brought him any food or drink. He waited and waited some more, and still the villagers went on with their eating and drinking without offering any to Pariacaca. This went on all day until finally one of the village women noticed poor Pariacaca sitting there and said, "Oh, this is shameful! You have been given nothing to eat or drink! How long have you been waiting?" And so, she filled a large cup to the brim with maize beer and brought it to him.

"Thank you for the drink, Sister," said Pariacaca. "Because you have been kind to me where others have not, I will tell you an important secret. Five days from now, there will be a terrible tragedy here in this village. I am angry with all the people here, but not with you, and I don't want to kill you and your family by mistake. If you want to live, take your family and go far, far away from here. I'm letting you know this because you have been kind to me, but if you breathe a word to anyone else here, you will be killed as well."

Five days later, the villagers still sat at their feast, eating and drinking, but the woman left the village with her husband and her children. Also, their other relations went with them, and so that family was spared the disaster that was to come.

And this was how the disaster came to be: Pariacaca was angered that the villagers had not given him the hospitality due to a stranger and a guest, so he went up to the top of the mountain that stood over the village. There he caused it to rain. Sheets of rain came down in heavy, great drops, and soon the earth at the top of the mountain was so heavy and wet that it slid down the mountainside and into the village. The mudslide came crashing down and swept away all the houses and all the animals and all the villagers. The whole village was washed right into the sea.

Near to the Yunca village that was destroyed by the mudslide was a place called Cupara, and in Cupara, they were suffering from drought. They had had no rain, and the channels for bringing water to their fields were drying up. The maize was dying in the fields, and there was nothing anyone could do about it.

Pariacaca came to Cupara, and there he saw a woman named Chuqui Suso working in her maize field. She was trying to water the maize by hand and weeping because she knew that she could not give the plants enough water no matter how hard she worked, and she was sure that she would die of hunger. Chuqui Suso was very beautiful, and Pariacaca desired her greatly. Pariacaca saw that Chuqui Suso's fields were being watered by a little pond nearby, so he stopped the mouth of the channel there with his cloak and caused the water to stop flowing entirely. Then he went to the woman and asked her why she was sorrowing so.

"I do not have enough water for my maize plants," she said, "and I do not know what I shall do."

"Yes, that is troublesome indeed," said Pariacaca, "but I can give you plenty of water if you sleep with me."

"I will let you sleep with me after you make the water flow," said the woman, "and after I see that my field has enough water."

"Very well," said Pariacaca.

Then Pariacaca removed his cloak from the mouth of the channel. He also increased the flow of water, and soon the field was very well watered indeed. Chuqui Suso rejoiced to see that her maize would now grow well.

"Let's sleep together now," said Pariacaca.

"Not yet," said the woman. "I think it would be better to wait. Maybe tomorrow."

"What if I make a channel that goes from the river to your fields? Then you will never lack for water ever again. Will you sleep with me if I do that for you?"

"Yes, I certainly will sleep with you then," said Chuqui Suso. "Dig the channel from the river, and we can sleep together when it is finished."

"Very well," said Pariacaca.

All sorts of animals came to help dig that canal. There were pumas and foxes, serpents and birds, and they all worked together. But before they started, they decided to choose a leader to direct the work. All the animals wanted to be the leader, but they finally decided that the fox would be best.

Under the direction of the fox, the animals began work on the watercourse. When it was halfway done, the fox accidentally flushed a tinamou bird from its covert. This startled the fox so badly that he jumped in the air and yelped, and then he fell halfway down the mountainside.

"We cannot work under such a leader," said the other animals. "He gets frightened by the smallest things. Let's have the snake be in charge now."

The snake took charge of the work, and soon the new channel was all finished and directing a fine flow of water into Chuqui Suso's maize field.

Pariacaca then went to Chuqui Suso and said, "I have carried out my promise. Your fields now have a good source of water. Your maize plants will grow and yield a fine harvest. Will you now keep your promise to me?"

"Yes, certainly," said Chuqui Suso. "Let's climb up to that high place. There we can sleep together very well."

And so Pariacaca and Chuqui Suso went to the high place she showed him, and there they slept together. When that was done, Chuqui Suso said, "Let's go to a different place."

Pariacaca agreed, and so they started off down the mountainside. They came to a place called Coco Challa, where the mouth of the canal that watered Chuqui Suso's fields was. When they came to the edge of the canal, Chuqui Suso cried out, "I'll go no farther! I will stay here in the mouth of my canal and never go anywhere else!"

With that, Chuqui Suso turned herself to stone, and there she stands to this very day.

## The Combat of Pariacaca and Huallallo Carhuincho

*The Andes Mountains are the highest mountains in the world outside of Asia. They are also part of the Pacific Ring of Fire and thus are home to several active volcanoes, which are created by the motion of the South American tectonic plate against the Nazca Plate. In the story retold below, we see a traditional conflict between a fire being (probably an anthropomorphized volcano) and a water being who can bring rain, hail, and mudslides.*

Once there was a *huaca* named Huallallo Carhuincho. This *huaca* was a fearsome creature made of fire. He ruled over the people, commanding them to have no more than two children and that one of the children must be given to him to eat. The people were greatly afraid of Huallallo, but they had no power to make him go away or to stop eating their children.

Pariacaca knew that Huallallo had been terrorizing the people and eating their children. They set out to find Huallallo and to defeat him, so that the people could live in peace.

Now, Pariacaca was not one single being but five. Pariacaca emerged from five condor eggs, first in the shape of five great condors who then took on human form and wandered about the world. The five Pariacacas met together at Ocsa Pata. They took their bolas and swirled them around, faster and faster. When Pariacaca swung the bolas, freezing cold and a great rain of hail came into that place.

While Pariacaca was swinging his bolas, a man came up the mountainside. The man carried an infant in one arm and a bundle of offerings in the other, and he was weeping very sorrowfully. Pariacaca saw the man and stopped swinging his bolas. "Friend," said Pariacaca, "why is it that you weep so?"

"Sir," said the man, "I am taking my child to Huallallo Carhuincho, for that *huaca* has commanded that we have no more than two children and that we give him one of the two to eat. Otherwise he will destroy us. I am taking this child to Huallallo to be his food, and this is why I weep."

Pariacaca was angered when he heard this. "Do not take your child to Huallallo. Take him back to your village. Give me your bundle of offerings. I will go to Huallallo and defeat him, and then you and your people can live in peace with all your children.

"I will fight with Huallallo in five days. You must come here and watch the combat. I will fight Huallallo with water, and he will fight me with fire. If I am winning, you must call out, 'Our father surely will be victorious!' But if Huallallo seems to be winning, you must declare the fight to be finished."

At first, the man refused to do as Pariacaca said. "I cannot do this thing. Huallallo surely will be angry with me."

"Don't worry about him," said Pariacaca. "I will deal with Huallallo, and you will be safe."

Finally, the day came for Pariacaca to fight with Huallallo. The five beings that were Pariacaca sent down rain upon Huallallo from five directions. They flashed lightning bolts at Huallallo from five directions.

Huallallo roared up in a great column of fire. No matter how much rain Pariacaca sent, the flame of Huallallo could not be extinguished. In this manner, Huallallo and Pariacaca fought all day long, and neither of them was able to get the better of the other, and the water from the rains of Pariacaca rushed down the mountainside and flowed all the way into the sea.

Finally, one of Pariacaca's selves, the one named Llacsa Churapa, knocked down a mountain and blocked the flow of water. Soon a lake had formed behind the dam. Huallallo was caught in the rising waters behind the dam. His fire was very nearly extinguished, and all the time Pariacaca was still hurling lightning at him, never stopping once to give his enemy any respite.

Huallallo saw that he would never be able to defeat Pariacaca, so he ran away down the mountain into the lowlands. The Pariacaca known as Paria Carco followed Huallallo and set himself at the foot of the mountain pass so that Huallallo would never be able to return. Also, Pariacaca commanded that Huallallo should never again eat children but eat only dogs from then on.

Now, Huallallo Carhuincho had a companion, a woman named Mama Ñamca. Like Huallallo, Mama Ñamca was a being all made of flame. Pariacaca knew that he would also have to defeat Mama Ñamca if his victory were to be complete, so he went to Tumna where he knew Mama Ñamca would be. One of Pariacaca's children, Chuqui Huampo, went with him.

Mama Ñamca saw Pariacaca coming. She knew that he was coming to do battle with her, and so she hurled a weapon at him, but it hit Chuqui Huampo instead. Pariacaca went to Mama Ñamca and fought with her. He defeated her and threw her into the sea.

Once Mama Ñamca was defeated, Pariacaca went back to Chuqui Huampo. Chuqui Huampo was now lame because Mama Ñamca's blow had broken his foot. "I cannot walk properly," said Chuqui Huampo, "so I'll stay here and make sure that Mama Ñamca doesn't come back."

Pariacaca agreed this was a good plan. Chuqui Huampo stayed in that place, and Pariacaca made sure that his child had enough food to sustain him. Pariacaca also said that the people of that place were to bring a tribute of coca leaves every year and to sacrifice a llama that had not yet borne young in Chuqui Huampo's honor.

And thus it was that Pariacaca defeated Huallallo Carhuincho and Mama Ñamca.

# PART II: INCA POLITICAL MYTHS

## The Tale of Manco Capac

*Transformation of an actual historical personage into a larger-than-life mythical character is a common process in many cultures, a process that the Incas also apparently embraced in their stories about Manco Capac, the founder and first ruler of the Inca state. Subsequent rulers, who used the name "Inca" as a royal title, traced their lineage and their claims to the throne back to this mytho-historical figure.*

*Although Manco Capac may have been an actual historical personage who ruled Cuzco, probably in the early thirteenth century, his story became embroidered into a political myth. There are several versions of this story which were compiled by Spanish redactors from Inca witnesses during the early colonial period. All of these versions of the tale assert some kind of divine origin for Manco Capac and his companions, as well as a variety of superhuman abilities that allow them to conquer the peoples in the various places they make their home on their way to founding the Inca capital city of Cuzco.*

Long, long ago, in the place called Pacaric-tombo, which means "Tavern of the Dawn," there was a hill called Tambo-toco, which means "Window of the Tavern." And in the hill called Tambo-toco there was a cave that had three windows. One window was called Capac-toco, which is "Royal Window." The Royal Window was in the center of the three, and it was decorated with beautiful silver and gold. The other two windows were called Sutic-toco and Maras-toco, but the meanings of these names have been lost.

From this cave of three windows came the ancestors of the Incas and of other peoples. They arose within the cave, not having mothers or fathers. From the window called Sutic-toco came the people known as Tampus, and they made their homes in the lands about the hill. From the window called Maras-toco came the people known as Maras, and they dwelt in the lands around Cuzco. From the window called Capac-toco came four men and four women. They came from the Royal Window because they were the ancestors of the Incas, and the founders of that mighty empire. Some have said that these ancestors of the Incas were the children of none other than Inti, the god of the sun, and Mama Quilla, the goddess of the moon.

The people who emerged through the Royal Window were Ayar Manco and his wife, Mama Ocllo; Ayar Auca and his wife, Mama Raua; Ayar Cachi and his wife, Mama Huaco; and Ayar Uchu and his wife, Mama Cura. The men and women were all dressed very richly. Their clothing was made of finely woven wool decorated with gold. The men carried golden halberds, and the women carried all the things needed to prepare and serve meals, and these were also made all of gold.

When the four men and four women emerged from the cave, they looked about them for a place to make their homes. They walked along through the mountains until they came to a place called Huanacauri, which is near Cuzco, where they made their homes and began to grow potatoes. But they were not satisfied that this was the best place, so one day they went up to the top of a mountain to see whether they could find a better land.

When they got to the top of the hill, Ayar Cachi took a stone and put it in his sling. He flung the stone with all his might at a nearby hill. Such was the strength of Ayar Cachi's arm that the stone he threw plowed through the hill, and when the dust cleared, the men and women saw that there was a ravine in its place. Ayar Cachi took three more stones, and with these, he knocked down three more hills and plowed three more ravines.

Seeing this, the others began to worry that with his great strength Ayar Cachi might try to rule them as a lord. They therefore plotted to be rid of him forever. They went to Ayar Cachi and said, "O Our Brother, we have left many things of great value in our cave of origin, things that we will need for our new homes. Will you not go back and fetch them?"

"With a good will I will do this," said Ayar Cachi, and so he went back to the cave.

The others followed Ayar Cachi secretly, and when he had gone into the cave, they took a great stone and covered its mouth. Then they sealed the stone in place by bricking it in with a wall made of many other stones and mud for mortar so that Ayar Cachi would not be able to get out no matter how hard he tried. The three men and four women waited to see whether Ayar Cachi would be able to dislodge the stones and open the mouth of the cave. Soon enough, Ayar Cachi came to the walled-up cave mouth. He shouted and pounded on the stone but could not move it. Satisfied that Ayar Cachi would be confined in the cave forever, the three men and four women went back to their homes at Huanacauri. Since Mama Huaco no longer had a husband, she became a servant to Ayar Manco.

The three men and four women still had not found a suitable place to call their home. They climbed the hill at Huanacauri so that they might look out over all the lands below and see whether any of those places would be better. While they were on the top of the hill looking about, a rainbow came into the sky. The rainbow hovered over the end of the Valley of Cuzco. The Ayars and the Mamas saw the rainbow, and they looked down into the valley.

"This is a good sign," said Ayar Manco. "We should go to the place marked by the rainbow and there make our homes."

The others agreed with this plan, but before they could begin their descent into the valley, a wondrous thing happened. A great pair of wings sprouted from the back of Ayar Uchu. The feathers were long and of many beautiful colors that shone in the light. As the others watched, Ayar Uchu spread his wings and flew up to the Sun. Ayar Manco, Ayar Auca, and the women waited, hoping that Ayar Uchu would come back. They waited for a long time, and just as they had begun to think their brother was lost to them forever, Ayar Uchu returned.

"Have no fear!" said Ayar Uchu. "I have spoken with our Father, the Sun, and he has bid me bring you tidings. He says that you are go into the Valley of Cuzco, where you shall found a new city that will be the beginning of a mighty empire, the empire of the Incas. There you are also to build temples to the Sun, that he might receive the worship and honor that is his due.

"Our Father the Sun says also that Ayar Manco is henceforth to be known as Manco Capac, The Supreme Rich One, for he is to become the founder of the empire and the ancestor of all the great Incas who are to come. Go now into the valley, and begin the work our Father the Sun has bid you to do!"

When Ayar Uchu finished speaking, he was turned into stone. Although Ayar Uchu's family did not mind his transformation, the other people who lived near the hill were frightened to see a stone idol with great wings flying about in the sky. One day, the people threw stones at the idol Ayar Uchu had become. The stones broke off one of his wings so he could no longer fly. He came to earth and the place where he landed became a *huaca*, a sacred place for honoring the gods.

Leaving the idol of Ayar Uchu behind, Manco Capac, his brother Ayar Auca, and the women began their journey into the Valley of Cuzco. Along the way, they took a rod of gold that belonged to Manco Capac and pressed it into the ground. Wherever they went, they found that the rod would not go more than a little way into the soil. By this sign they knew that they had not yet reached the place they were to settle. They journeyed on to a place farther along the valley, testing the soil with the rod all the while. When they were not far from the place where they were to build the city of Cuzco, they thrust the rod into the ground. This time, the ground did not resist at all; instead, it yielded so readily that the rod was quickly swallowed up and buried in the soil. Then the Ayars and Mamas knew they had reached the place that they were to settle, the place in which they were to begin to found their empire.

Manco Capac looked about this new land, and not far off he saw a pile of stones. "Go and look at those stones," he told Ayar Auca.

"With a good will I will do it," said Ayar Auca, who then sprouted a pair of wings just as Ayar Uchu had done and then flew off to the place where the stones were.

Ayar Auca found that the pile of stones was in a place where two streams met in their courses. Flying down, he lit upon one of the stones and there was transformed into stone himself. This was to signify that the place now belonged to the Ayars and the Mamas, and on that spot was built the Temple of the Sun.

Manco Capac traveled onward to Matagua with the three women. By this time, Mama Ocllo had given birth to a fine son, whose name was Sinchi Roca. When their settlement had been built there beneath the peak of Huanacauri, they celebrated for Sinchi Roca the rite called *huarachico*, wherein the ears of the children of the nobility are pierced for the first time, for it is a sign of nobility to wear plugs in the earlobes. They also celebrated the feast of Capac Raymi, the great dance that is made for the turning of the year at the summer solstice, to honor Inti, the god of the sun.

After two years at Matagua, Manco Capac and the women decided that it was time for them to seek a better place to live. To find out which way they should go, Mama Huaco took two golden rods and threw them northwards. Mama Huaco was very strong, and the rods went a very long way. One landed in a place where the land had not been terraced. That rod did not sink into the ground. The other rod landed in a field near Cuzco and firmly planted itself in the soil there. Manco Capac and the women knew that the place near Cuzco would be the best for them to live in for the land there was tilled and fertile.

They went to that land near Cuzco, but when they arrived, they found it was already inhabited by people who grew coca and hot peppers. Those people resisted the coming of Manco Capac until Mama Huaco took her sling and killed one of them. Then Mama Huaco sliced open his body, removed the lungs, and then blew into them, making them swell up. This she showed to the inhabitants of that place, whereupon they all fled, leaving the land for Manco Capac and the women to have for their own.

There it was that Manco Capac and the women settled. They tilled the soil and planted the seeds of maize that they had brought with them when they left the caves. They built a temple to the Sun, which they called the House of the Sun. And they spread their power over the land, going forth from time to time and conquering neighboring peoples. And when Manco Capac was a very old man and his son Sinchi Roca came to manhood, Manco Capac handed the title of Inca to his son so that Sinchi Roca might rule.

And thus it was that the empire of the Incas began, long, long ago.

# The Tale of Mayta Capac

*In addition to the foundation myth that was intended to grant the Inca political legitimacy, other stories about subsequent Incas also paint them as larger-than-life beings with special powers and divine or semi-divine origins. Here we have the story of Inca Lloque Yupanqui's wish for an heir, which is granted by none other than the Sun himself. Although the story asserts that Lloque Yupanqui was the father of Mayta Capac, the connection to a divine origin is maintained by the prodigious growth of the young lad, who is already large and strong enough to defeat trained youths and even grown men when he is only two years old.*

*This story also speaks of Mayta Capac "taking the fringe." Imperial power in the Inca Empire was symbolized by a braided chaplet topped with feathers to which was attached a long fringe made of fine, red wool decorated with gold. "Taking the fringe" therefore is the Inca equivalent to the Western idea of coronation as conveying absolute power.*

The grandson of Manco Capac was Lloque Yupanqui, and he ruled wisely and well as the third Inca. But for a long time, Lloque Yupanqui remained unmarried, and so he came into his old age without an heir. One day as he sat sorrowing over his plight, he had a vision of the Sun, who told him that he would surely father a fine son who would be a worthy successor to the throne.

Lloque Yupanqui therefore began to search for a bride among the daughters of the lords of the empire. He found one in the town of Oma, a woman by the name of Mama Caua. Lloque Yupanqui asked whether Mama Caua might become his wife, and her father gladly granted his assent. The Inca Lloque and the family of Mama Caua were very pleased with this match. Mama Caua was a very beautiful woman, and her marriage to the Inca himself was a source of great pride for her and her family.

When the match was announced, there was a great feast held in Oma to celebrate the departure of Mama Caua for Cuzco. And all along the road, there was much feasting and dancing and rejoicing, for the Inca had commanded that his marriage be a time of rejoicing for all his people. Finally, Mama Caua arrived in Cuzco. The Inca himself came to the gate of the city to meet her with all his nobles in his train. They greeted her well and made her very welcome, and the whole city rejoiced with feasting and dancing for many days.

As the Sun had promised, Mama Caua soon found herself with child, and the baby was given the name Mayta Capac. But this was no ordinary child: Mayta was born fully formed after only three months. When he opened his mouth to give his first cry, everyone saw that he already had all his teeth. He grew so quickly that at the end of his first year, he was as tall as an eight-year-old child, and by the time he was two, he was so strong and so skilled at games and feats of arms that he could defeat young men who were much bigger and older than he.

One time, he went to play at rough games with young men from the Alcabisas and Culunchimas, tribes who lived near Cuzco. The youths could not stop Mayta. He wrought havoc amongst them, injuring many and killing a few others. On another day, Mayta and the other youths of the Alcabisas went to slake their thirst at a fountain. A dispute broke out over who had the right to drink first. Mayta broke the leg of the son of the chief of the Alcabisas, and when the other lads fled, he chased them down until they ran into their houses and barred the doors against him.

The chiefs of the Alcabisas and Culunchimas saw how badly Mayta Capac had abused their sons. Surely a child that was so very large and strong at the age of two would be an unstoppable foe once he reached his full growth and manhood. The Alcabisas therefore proposed to rid themselves of both the old Inca and Mayta Capac together. They sent their most skilled men to the House of the Sun in Cuzco with orders to find the Inca and his son and kill them. When the men arrived, Mayta Capac was in the forecourt of the House, playing ball with some of his friends. Mayta saw the approach of his enemies. He took the ball he had been playing with and hurled it at the foremost man. It hit him in the forehead and killed him instantly. Mayta Capac took up the ball as it bounced back to him and threw it at another man, killing him likewise. He then set upon the rest, and although they managed to escape with their lives, not one of them was unwounded.

The Alcabisas and Culunchimas saw how handily Mayta Capac had defeated their finest picked men, and they were very afraid. They therefore summoned together all their warriors into a great army, thinking to attack Cuzco and take it for their own and dispose of the Inca and his wayward son in the bargain, for surely even Mayta Capac would not be able to hold off an entire army. Word of the impending battle reached the ears of Inca Lloque Yupanqui. He called to him his son and said, "What then have you done that the people rise up in rebellion against me? You have called down a bad fate upon me, and I shall die at the hands of rebels."

"Fear not, O Father," said Mayta Capac. "The warriors of the Inca are mighty, and we will defeat this foe."

Inca Lloque Yupanqui protested, for he did not want war to come to his kingdom, but he was overruled by Mayta Capac and by his own nobles, who wanted to obtain glory for themselves by defeating the Alcabisas and Culunchimas.

Soon enough, the armies of the Inca and the Alcabisas and Culunchimas met on the field of battle. Both armies fought hard and well, but in the end, the army of the Inca was victorious. But the Alcabisas and Culunchimas could not be dissuaded from their attempt to unseat the Inca and slay his mighty son. Again, they challenged Mayta Capac and his army to battle, and again, they were defeated. The chief of the Alcabisas was taken in that battle and spent the rest of his life as the captive of Mayta Capac.

After the death of Inca Lloque Yupanqui, Mayta Capac took up the imperial fringe, becoming the fourth Inca. Also, Mayta Capac had in his possession a magical bird that had been brought from the cave of Tambo-toco by Manco Capac. Mayta Capac was able to understand the speech of this bird which could see the future. Many times, Mayta Capac took counsel of the magical bird and used its oracles to determine what courses to take in his rule. Mayta Capac stayed in Cuzco for the duration of his reign, and when he died, the fringe passed to his son, Capac Yupanqui.

## Topa Inca Yupanqui and Macahuisa

*Topa Inca Yupanqui ruled the empire between 1471 and 1493. He headed the Inca army under his father, Pachacuti, and was involved in a significant expansion of Inca territory. This story mythologizes one of his conquests, legitimizing his rule over the conquered peoples by asserting divine assistance given to Topa Inca Yupanqui's armies.*

Topa Inca Yupanqui was a very powerful king. He went up and down the land, conquering all manner of people and bringing them under the rule of the Inca. For a long time after those conquests, there was peace and prosperity, but one day three peoples—the Allancu, the Callancu, and the Chaqui—decided they had had enough of Inca rule, and they rose up against Inca Yupanqui.

Inca Yupanqui mustered his armies. He sent them out to fight against these three peoples. But no matter how many men he sent, and no matter how skilled his warriors were, they were not able to reconquer those peoples. The battles went on and on for a full twelve years, and at the end of that time, Inca Yupanqui began to despair of ever having victory. He thought to himself, "I offer all manner of good things to the *huacas*, to the divine spirits that protect my people. The *huacas* have silver. They have gold. They have the best food and the finest raiment. Surely if I call upon them, they will come to my aid!"

And so, Inca Yupanqui went out, and he summoned all the *huacas*. He commanded them to come to his aid if they had received rich gifts from him. He bade them to meet in the plaza at the center of Cuzco where he would take counsel with them and find out what remedies they might offer against his enemies.

The *huacas* heard the call of Inca Yupanqui. They came from the villages and the mountains all around, riding in litters carried by their retainers. Even the mighty Pachacamac was there. But Pariacaca didn't want to go. He delayed and delayed, but finally he knew he could wait no more. If he did not go himself, some representative of his house must go. So Pariacaca called to himself his son, Macahuisa, and told him to go to the meeting and see what must be done.

Macahuisa obeyed Pariacaca. He went on his litter to the meeting in Cuzco. He sat at the edge of the meeting and listened to what Inca Yupanqui had to say.

"O my Fathers, mighty *huacas*, great *villcas*! O gods, divine beings, and spirits of the mountains! I have served you ever, with rich gifts of gold and silver, of the best food and the finest raiment. Never have I stinted you. Since I have given you all those things, will you not come to my aid?"

But the *huacas* and the other spirit beings said nothing.

"Tell me, why do you not answer? The people who serve me and who serve you are daily being slaughtered by our enemies. Many thousands already have we lost. Answer me, or I shall have you all burned!"

Again, the *huacas* and the other beings kept their peace. Inca Yupanqui grew angry and impatient. He said, "I have served you well and given you of my wealth. Gold and silver and sacrifices of many llamas have been yours. Now that I stand before you and ask for something in return, you sit there silent as though you know me not! Will you not aid me? Will you not aid my people? Speak, or I shall have you all burned!"

Finally, the great Pachacamac spoke. "O Inca Yupanqui, O Sun in the Sky, I would help you if I could, but my power is so great that if I shook your enemies to destroy them, you and your people would be destroyed as well. If I put forth my might in that way, it might even end the whole world. I do wish to help you, but I cannot. That is why I have not spoken."

Then there was another silence. Not one of the other *huacas* spoke. Inca Yupanqui despaired that any of them would offer help at all until finally Macahuisa said, "O Inca, O Sun in the Sky, I will help you. If you stay here and protect your people, I will go forth and conquer your enemies. I shall do this thing right away!"

As Macahuisa spoke, a green-blue vapor issued from his mouth that looked like smoke. Then Macahuisa took up his panpipes and clad himself in his finest raiment. The Inca commanded that a litter be prepared for Macahuisa with the fastest, strongest bearers in all the kingdom so that Macahuisa might come to the battlefield as soon as may be.

Macahuisa went to the place where the enemies of Inca Yupanqui lived. There Macahuisa caused it to rain. The rain came down gently at first, soft and grey. But then the rain grew heavier and stronger. The wind rose. Thunder rumbled across the sky, and forked lightning split the air. The thunder and lightning grew, and the rain grew heavier yet. Soon all the enemies of the Inca were washed away by the torrent of water, but Macahuisa let a few of them escape the flood to take back to Inca Yupanqui as prisoners and proof of his conquest.

When Inca Yupanqui saw that Macahuisa had thus conquered all his enemies, he vowed unending gratitude to Pariacaca for sending his son to help him and gave him fifty attendants to see to his needs and offer him the best sacrifices. Then Inca Yupanqui bowed down in thanks to Macahuisa, saying, "I owe you a great debt, O Macahuisa, for you came to my aid and conquered my enemies. Whatever you ask of me, this shall I do."

Macahuisa replied, "I wish for nothing, save that you worship me in the same way that the Yauyo people do."

Inca Yupanqui replied, "Yes, certainly!" but in his heart he was afraid because perhaps Macahuisa might deal with him the way he had done with the Inca's enemies.

Then the Inca called for food to be brought to Macahuisa, but the *huaca* said, "Oh, I do not eat food such as you eat. Bring to me instead the shells of thorny oysters."

The Inca sent for thorny oyster shells and gave them to Macahuisa. The *huaca* ate them hungrily, all in one bite, crunching and crunching the hard shells.

When Macahuisa was done eating, the Inca said, "We have here many beautiful maidens who would be honored to share your bed. Please choose from among them, as many as you wish!"

Macahuisa replied, "That is most generous of you, but I do not require their services."

Then Macahuisa bade farewell to Inca Yupanqui, and he went back home to tell his father Pariacaca of all that had happened during his sojourn in the land of the Incas.

And from that time forward, the Inca Yupanqui and his successors worshipped Macahuisa, dancing special dances in his honor, and the Inca himself led the dancing in gratitude for what the *huaca* had done for him and his people.

## Inca Huayna Capac and Coniraya

*This story from the Huarochirí Manuscript is a myth woven around an actual historical personage. The Inca Huayna Capac lived from c. 1464/68 to c. 1525/27 and was the successor to Topa Inca Yupanqui. Conquests achieved during Huayna Capac's reign extended the empire north into Ecuador and Colombia and south into Chile and Argentina. Huayna Capac was the last Inca to rule independently before the arrival of the Spanish.*

Not long before the Spanish came to Cuzco, Coniraya decided to go and visit the Inca Huayna Capac. Coniraya went to the Inca and said, "Let us go to Lake Titicaca. I have some things to show you there."

And so Huayna Capac went with Coniraya to Titicaca. When they arrived, Coniraya said, "Summon your magicians and sages. We must send them to the underworld."

"I shall do as you ask," said Huayna Capac.

Soon the magicians and sages started to arrive.

"I am the sage of the condor!" said one.

"I am the sage of the hawk!" said another.

A third one said, "I am the sage of the swallow!"

Coniraya addressed the sages, saying, "You must go to the underworld. There you must ask my father to send one of my sisters to me."

The sages said that they would do as Coniraya asked, and they set out on their road. The first to arrive in the underworld was the sage of the swallow. He told Coniraya's father the message he bore. Coniraya's father gave the sage of the swallow a small chest and told him, "Do not open this. It is for Inca Huayna Capac and no other man."

The man took the chest and left the underworld. Now, it was a long journey back to Titicaca, and the whole way along the road the sage of the swallow burned with curiosity over what the chest contained. Finally, he could bear it no longer. He opened the chest and saw inside it a beautiful maiden with long golden hair and the finest raiment. Because she was inside the chest, she appeared to be very small. But when she saw the sage looking at her, she disappeared!

The sage of the swallow was very frightened. He did not want to go back to Titicaca. He did not want to admit that he had opened the chest that was only for Inca Huayna Capac. But the sage was an honest man, and so he went before the Inca and confessed what he had done.

When Huayna Capac heard the sage's tale, he shouted, "I would have you killed on the spot if you were not the sage of the swallow! Go back to the underworld! And this time bring back the chest without opening it!"

And so, the sage of the swallow returned to the underworld, and again he received the chest. This time, he did not open it on his road. On and on he walked, on the long journey back to Titicaca, and at day's end, he found himself still a long way from any village, and he was very hungry and tired. "Oh, how I wish I had a nice meal and a soft bed!" the sage said to himself.

Suddenly, a table appeared before the sage, laid with a tasty meal. The sage sat down and ate gratefully, and when he was done, the table and the dishes all vanished, and in their place a soft bed appeared. The sage lay down on the bed and slept deeply and well. And so, it went for the five days of his journey back to Titicaca: when he was hungry, the table would appear, filled with good things to eat; when he was tired, the bed would appear, and he would take his rest.

On the fifth day, the sage arrived at Titicaca and went before Inca Huayna Capac and Coniraya. "O Inca, Sun in the Sky," said the sage, "here is the chest that Coniraya's father sent you."

Before Huayna Capac could open the chest, Coniraya said, "Wait! Let us divide the world between us. I'll go to this part. You can go to this part with my sister. You and I cannot be in the same place together."

Then Huayna Capac opened the chest. A brilliant light shone out of it, and out stepped the beautiful woman.

"I will not return to Cuzco," said Huayna Capac. "I will stay here with my beautiful new wife. You!" he said, pointing to one of his kinsmen, "you will return to Cuzco. You will say, 'I am Huayna Capac,' and you will rule in my stead."

Then Huayna Capac and his beautiful wife vanished from that place, and so did Coniraya, and none of them were ever seen again. The man who pretended to be Huayna Capac went back to Cuzco where he ruled as Inca. But when he died, the people quarreled about who was to lead them next. And it was while they were fighting thus that the Spanish arrived.

# PART III: FIVE ANDEAN FOLKTALES AND AN INCA PLAY

## The Macaw Woman

*The legend of the Macaw Woman is the origin tale of the Cañari people, who hail from an area of southern Ecuador. The Cañari were conquered by the Incas and absorbed into the empire in the sixteenth century, not long before the arrival of the Spanish.*

Once there was a great flood. The waters rose and rose. They filled the valleys. They climbed up the hills. Soon they reached nearly to the top of the mountains. All the animals and people were drowned, all except for two brothers who managed to climb all the way up to the top of a mountain. There they waited until the flood waters receded, and when they deemed it safe, they went down the mountainside until they found a place that suited them, and there they built a home for themselves.

Every day, the brothers left their home to forage for food. Because the flood had destroyed everything, they could only find various roots and a few herbs to eat. It was but poor fare, and they barely found enough to live on, even though they worked very hard every day.

One day, the brothers returned home after a long day spent foraging to find that someone had lit a fire inside their home, and a meal of good cooked food and maize beer set out on the table. Not waiting to find out who might have given them such bounty, the brothers sat down immediately. They ate every last morsel and drank every last drop, and when they were finished, they collapsed into their beds, content for the first time in many, many months.

The next day, the brothers went out foraging as usual, and when they returned home, they again found their table laid with choice food and drink. This went on for ten days.

Finally, the elder brother said, "Who do you think it is that lays such a table for us every night?"

"I'm sure I don't know," said the younger brother. "I should like to thank them, but they seem not to want us to see them."

"I want to know who it is," said the elder. "Tomorrow, instead of going foraging, I will hide inside the house. I will wait to see who it is that leaves a good meal for us every day. I am tired of living with this mystery."

In the morning, the younger brother went out to search for food, but the elder hid himself in a corner of the house. Soon enough, two women came into the house. But these were not ordinary women: they were actually macaws, and they were the most beautiful beings the elder brother had ever seen.

The macaw women moved about the house, lighting the fire and setting things ready to cook the meal. The elder brother could stand it no longer; he jumped out of his hiding place and tried to catch one of the women. The macaw women were frightened. They evaded his grasp, turned back into macaws, and flew away, leaving no meal for the brothers that evening.

The younger brother came home and found that no food had been prepared. The elder explained what had happened, that he had tried to capture one of the macaw women but failed.

"Tomorrow I shall watch with you," said the younger brother. "Perhaps together we can capture one of the women."

The next day, the brothers hid themselves inside the house, but the macaw women did not return. The brothers continued to keep their vigil, hoping that the women would come back. Finally, at the end of the third day, the macaw women appeared and set to work preparing a meal. This time, the brothers waited until the meal was ready. When all had been placed on the table, they jumped out of their hiding place. The women were angry and frightened and turned back into birds. The younger brother ran to bar the door so that the birds could not escape. The elder brother managed to catch one of the birds, but the other escaped out the window.

The macaw changed back into a woman. She became the wife of both of the brothers and bore them six sons and six daughters. She also had brought with her many seeds which the brothers planted as crops and harvested at their proper times. And so, the human race had a new start, there on the sacred mountain, and all people are the descendants of the macaw woman and her twelve children.

## The Condor and the Shepherdess

*The Aymara people live in parts of what are now Peru, Bolivia, and Chile, and were absorbed into the Inca Empire in the early sixteenth century during the reign of Huayna Capac. This Aymara folktale shows the importance of the condor to Andean peoples. Some versions of this tale also function as a just-so story for the origin of hummingbirds: instead of many smaller parrots being created out of a greater one at the end of the tale, hummingbirds result instead.*

Once there was a shepherdess who would go out onto the mountainside every day to graze her flock. She liked being out of doors, feeling the wind in her hair and the grass and stones under her boots. She also liked being alone, for when she was out with her flock, no one could tell her what to do or speak to her when she did not feel like talking.

Near that same mountain there lived a condor. Every day he would fly out looking for food to eat. He frequently soared over the place where the shepherdess grazed her sheep, and at first, he took no notice of her, for he knew that when a guardian was present, he would not be able to steal a lamb very easily, and he preferred not to have to work too hard for his food. But one day, the shepherdess happened to look up as the condor sailed past. The condor caught a glimpse of her face and instantly fell in love with her. "What shall I do?" he lamented. "She is a beautiful young woman, and I am a great, ugly bird. She will never consent to be my bride."

The condor pined for many days, wondering how to go about getting the young woman to marry him. Then he hit upon it: he would change his form. He would take on the shape of a handsome young man, and then she would surely wish to be his wife. And so, the very next day the condor watched to see whether the shepherdess would take her flock to graze on the mountainside, and when she did, the condor alit on the ground out of sight and turned himself into a young man.

The condor walked over to where the young woman was watching her sheep. He greeted her well and asked, "What is it you are doing out here on the mountainside all alone?"

"I am watching my sheep," she answered. "I keep the foxes and the condors away, and I make sure my sheep get enough good grass to eat."

"Don't you ever get lonely with only the sheep to keep you company?" said the condor.

"Oh, no, never!" said the young woman. "I like being here by myself."

"Well, maybe someday you might change your mind," said the condor. "Perhaps I could help you. I'm good at chasing away foxes and condors. How would you like to have me for a husband?"

"No, thank you," said the young woman. "I don't want to marry anyone. I want to live alone and raise my sheep."

"Very well," said the condor, and then he walked away.

The next day, the condor again took the form of a man and talked with the shepherdess.

"How would you like to come and live with me?" he asked. "I live up at the very top of the mountains. I see the sunrise and the sunset. Sometimes I am even above the clouds. It is very quiet and peaceful where I live. Are you sure you don't want to be my wife? I think you would like my home very much."

"Thank you, but no," said the shepherdess. "I really do not want to get married at all. I prefer to stay here with my sheep, and besides, if I left my mother would be very sad."

"That's all right then" said the condor. "But before I go, do you think you might scratch the itch between my shoulder blades? It bothers me so, and I cannot reach it myself."

"Certainly," said the young woman. She went to the condor and began to scratch the spot between his shoulder blades, but as she did so, he turned back into a condor and flew up into the sky, pulling the woman up with him on his back. The condor flew high up into the mountains, and he did not stop flying until he reached a place where there were many caves. He alighted inside one of them, where his mother lived. The other condors in the nearby caves came out to see who had arrived, and when they saw that the condor had brought a young woman back with him, they danced and flapped their wings for joy.

At first, the young woman was very happy living with the condor because he loved her very much. But soon she began to feel cold and hungry and thirsty. "I cannot stay here like this," she said. "I need fire and food and water, and I see none of that here. If I do not get those things, I will die."

"Do not worry, my love," said the condor. "I will bring everything you need."

The condor flew away from the cave. He circled down toward the valley. He found a place where a fire was burning low on the hearth and no one about to tend it. The condor picked up a coal in his beak and brought it back to the cave so that his wife could build a fire. Then he went to a place in the mountainside near his cave and dug at the rock with his beak. Soon a spring of fresh water leaped out, and his wife was able to drink. That done, the condor went back down into the valley. He collected up pieces of meat from dead animals. He dug up potatoes from an untended field. The condor brought this food back to his bride, but the meat was rank and the potatoes were rotting. The young woman ate these things because there was nothing else and she was so very hungry, but the food was disgusting.

After a time, the young woman's body began to change. She became very thin from the cold and the bad food. Feathers began to sprout from her body, and her hair fell out. She even began to lay eggs. Although her husband was very loving and attentive, she began to feel restless and longed to go home to her mother.

Meanwhile, the young woman's mother was beside herself with worry and sorrow. Her daughter had not come home with the sheep as she usually did, and it was not until the morning after the condor had taken the shepherdess that a neighbor brought the flock back to the young woman's mother. The mother went out onto the mountainside to look for her daughter, but she found nothing, and no one could tell her where her child had gone. Many days passed until the poor woman began to wonder whether her daughter had died.

One morning, the mother sat weeping near an open window. A parrot was flying by and heard the poor woman sorrowing. The parrot flew in through the window and said, "Why do you weep so? What is it that makes you so sad?"

"My daughter has disappeared," said the mother, "and I do not know where she has gone. I do not know whether she is alive or dead, but I fear the worst."

"You need not fear," said the parrot. "Your daughter is alive and well. I know where she is. She has been taken to wife by the great condor. She lives with him in a cave high up in the mountains. If you will let me eat maize from your garden and nest in your trees, I will bring her back to you."

The mother readily agreed, and so the parrot flew away into the mountains. After a short time, he spied the cave where the young woman lived with her condor husband and their chicks. The parrot waited until the condors had all gone out looking for food, then he flew into the cave.

"Have no fear," said the parrot to the shepherdess. "I have come to take you home to your mother." Then the parrot picked up the shepherdess in his claws and flew back to the mother's house.

When the parrot arrived carrying the shepherdess, the mother cried out in sorrow to see how changed her daughter was. The shepherdess was so thin that her bones were peeking out through her skin, and she had feathers all over her body. She smelled very bad, and her hair had almost all fallen out. But the mother embraced her daughter tenderly and brought her into the house, where she bathed the young woman and gave her fresh, warm clothing to wear.

Later that day, the condor returned to his cave and found his wife had gone. "I know who did this," said the condor. "It was the parrot. I shall make him pay for his insolence."

The condor flew down to the mother's garden where the parrot had made a nest in a tree and where he was feasting on grains of maize.

Before the parrot even knew what was happening, the condor swooped down upon him and swallowed him whole. But the parrot did not die: he passed right through the condor's body and came out the other end. The condor was furious when he saw this. He captured the parrot again and swallowed him again, but the same thing happened: out came the parrot at the other end, quite alive. Then the condor grabbed the parrot in his claws and tore him to little shreds. He ate the shreds, one by one, but these merely passed through his body and came out the other end as small, lively parrots.

The condor realized he could never get his revenge on the parrot and that he never would be able to get his wife back. In great sorrow, he flew back to his mountain cave. He took ashes from the cold fireplace and painted them all over his feathers so that they turned black. He wept many tears as he did this, and those tears became the flecks of ash that float above fireplaces.

## The Maiden and the Three Warriors

*The story of the maiden and the three warriors explains how the town of Huanuco and three nearby peaks came to be. Huanuco is about 1,200 km (745 mi) north of Cuzco and lies in a valley through which flows the Huallaga River. Mount Runtuy, which the story says was named after Runtus, a warrior who vies for the hand of the maiden, is located in the Huayhuash range of the Andes, which runs to the west of Huanuco. (I have been unable to identify the locations of the other two peaks.)*

Once there was a chief named Pillco-Rumi who had fifty sons and but one daughter. The daughter's name was Cori-Huayta, which means "Golden Flower." She was well named for she was the most beautiful maiden anyone had ever seen, and she was the jewel of her father's heart. So well did Pillco-Rumi love Cori-Huayta that he vowed never to let her marry a mortal man. In this he was transgressing his own law which said that all maidens and young men must marry when they come of age. No one knew of the chief's vow, for he had never spoken of it to anyone, and so when young men from all around became enamored of Cori-Huayta, they told themselves that surely they would be the one chosen to be her husband.

Finally the time came when Cori-Huayta was of an age to marry. Pillco-Rumi went to the High Priest to take counsel on what was to be done.

"O High Priest," said Pillco-Rumi, "I do not wish my daughter to marry. You best know our laws; what might be done to keep her by my side?"

"Well you know the laws, O my chief," said the High Priest. "She may not stay with you. If she take not a mortal husband, then she must join the Daughters of the Sun in the House of the Sun and there spend her days in service to the Sun himself."

But still Pillco-Rumi insisted that there must be a third way, and still he vowed that Cori-Huayta would neither marry a mortal man nor become a Daughter of the Sun. And so Pillco-Rumi prayed to Inti, to the sun-god himself, saying, "O My Father the Sun, no mortal man is worthy of my daughter, and I would not have her spend her days confined to the House of the Sun. I ask that none but you be her husband, if you will have her."

No answer did Pillco-Rumi receive, and so he began preparations for the Spring Festival, at which all maidens and young men who were of age must marry, with a heavy heart.

Word had gone out to all the lands that Cori-Huayta was to be wed at the coming festival. Three warriors, each from a different land, gathered their armies and set out to march to the lands of Pillco-Rumi to see whether they might persuade her father to let her marry them.

The first of these warriors was named Runtus. He was an old man, and his hair had already turned white. "Surely Cori-Huayta will have me for a husband," he said, "for I am a man of age and wisdom, and I will be able to make her happy and care for her well."

The second was named Maray. He was a young man and exceptionally strong. No man had ever defeated him in battle. "I am the best husband for Cori-Huayta," said Maray. "Women are weak and need a strong man to protect them. I am the strongest by far, and therefore she should marry me."

Paucar was the name of the third man, and he was the handsomest man that had ever lived. Every maiden that saw him immediately fell in love with him, but he spurned them all. "Only Cori-Huayta is to be my bride," said Paucar, "for I will only wed the one who can match me in beauty."

On the day the festival was to begin, Cori-Huayta made herself ready, thinking that she was to be given a husband for her father had said nothing to her of his vow that she would never wed a mortal man. Pillco-Rumi, for his part, went to the city walls to pray once more to Inti, hoping that this time the god would hear him. As he walked the walls, Cori-Huayta came to stand with him. She saw that her father was troubled. "What is it, O My Father? What weighs upon your heart? Surely today should be a day of rejoicing," she said.

But Pillco-Rumi made no answer for at that moment he saw three great clouds of dust on the horizon. Soon he realized that these were three armies coming toward his city. As Pillco-Rumi and Cori-Huayta watched, three runners came to the walls, each one sent by his master. The first was from Runtus, the second from Maray, and the third from Paucar. Each of them said that their master was coming to claim the hand of Cori-Huayta, and that if she was not given over, that their army would sack the city and leave nothing alive within it.

"Armies approach!" cried Pillco-Rumi to his people who had gathered in the plaza below to make merry at the festival. "Pray! Pray to Inti that we should be spared!"

The people all immediately knelt and intreated the sun-god to spare them. While they prayed, a rainbow appeared in the sky above them.

Seated on the rainbow was Inti. He heard the prayers, and he saw the armies approaching Pillco-Rumi's city. Inti looked upon Paucar in his army and turned them all into a high mountain covered with snow. The snow melted under the heat of Inti's rays and rushed down the mountainside and into a channel, becoming a mighty river. Then Inti turned his gaze upon Maray and Runtus, likewise turning them and their armies into stone. And so where the three armies had been now stood three new mountains.

Then Inti looked down upon the city of Pillco-Rumi. He uttered a single word, "Huanucuy!" which rumbled through the air like thunder. And the meaning of that word is "Live no more upon the earth." When that word was uttered, Cori-Huayta fell down, dead. Inti stretched out his hand from the heavens and took her to himself to be his bride. And so it was that the daughter of Pillco-Rumi neither wed a mortal man nor became a Daughter of the Sun.

Today the three mountains Inti made bear the names of the warriors who sought to marry Cori-Huayta, and the city bears the name Huanuco after the word uttered by Inti when he took Cori-Huayta to be his bride.

## The Llama-Herder and the Daughter of the Sun

*The story of the llama-herder is found in a manuscript compiled in 1585 by Spanish missionary Fray Martín de Murúa (1525-1618). De Murúa says that the mountains spoken of at the end of the tale are between Calca and Huayllabamba. Both of these towns are just north of Cuzco, with Calca lying to the east and Huayllabamba to the west.*

Once there was a young llama-herder named Acoya-napa who lived in a town called Laris. Every day Acoya-napa would take his flock of llamas out onto the mountainside to graze, and there he would amuse himself by playing his panpipes while he watched over his flock. Not far from where the young man grazed his flock was the House of the Sun, where lived many young women from throughout the Inca Empire, along with their caretakers, and the duty of those who lived there was to ensure the proper worship of Inti, god of the sun. The young women who lived in the House of the Sun were known as the Daughters of the Sun, and it was a law that they were to remain unmarried for their whole duty was to conduct the worship of Inti and give thought to no others.

From time to time, some of the Daughters of the Sun would leave their temple and wander freely about the mountainside. This they were allowed to do as long as they returned by sundown and as long as they did not neglect their obligations within the House of the Sun.

One day, two Daughters of the Sun thought to go for a stroll about the mountainside together. They walked along companionably, enjoying the bright sunshine and the greenery of the fields. As they walked, they heard the lilting sound of panpipes being played nearby. They wondered who it was that played so skillfully, so they went toward the sound. Soon enough, they found Acoya-napa, seated on a large rock, playing his pipes while his llamas grazed. The young women hid themselves from Acoya-napa's view so he never had any inkling that someone was listening to him.

For many days thereafter, the two Daughters of the Sun went to that place to listen to the llama-herder play his music, and they did so in secret. But one day, one of the Daughters, whose name was Chuquillantu, had a mind to meet this young man who played so sweetly. She convinced her sister to go with her, and so they went to the rock where Acoya-napa was sitting and greeted him courteously.

Acoya-napa was overcome. He had never seen two such beautiful women in his life, clothed as they were in the raiment of the House of the Sun. The young llama-herder fell on his knees before them, certain that they were divine beings.

The women reassured the young man that they were not divine but human beings just like him. They raised Acoya-napa to his feet, and he kissed their hands, surprised to find that they were warm and solid, flesh and blood, just like him. Acoya-napa and the young women spoke for a little while together, but then he said it was time for him to guide his flock back to his home. The Daughters of the Sun gladly granted him leave to depart, and as he said goodbye to them, his eyes met those of Chuqui-llantu, and her heart was suddenly rent by a great love of this handsome young man who played so well upon his panpipes and who looked after his flock with such good care.

The young people went their separate ways, Acoya-napa to his home with his llamas, and the young women to the House of the Sun. When Chuqui-llantu and her sister arrived at the House of the Sun, they found their sisters preparing the evening meal. Chuqui-llantu excused herself, saying that she was tired and did not feel hungry. She went to her chamber and lay upon her bed, able to think of nothing but the handsome young llama-herder. Chuqui-llantu's sister, meanwhile, ate with the rest of the household, not knowing that Chuqui-llantu was smitten with love for Acoya-napa, for the sister had not seen in him anything very special at all.

Chuqui-llantu lay upon her bed pining for young Acoya-napa, but tired from her long day in the fresh air, she soon fell asleep, and while she was sleeping, she had a dream. In the dream, Chuqui-llantu saw a little songbird that was flitting from tree to tree, singing merrily. The bird saw Chuqui-llantu's sorrow and said, "Why do you weep so?"

"I weep for love," said Chuqui-llantu. "I weep because my heart pines for young Acoya-napa, and I know not what to do, for if I declare my love for him, it will be my fate to be killed. I am a Daughter of the Sun and may never marry."

The bird said, "Have no fear. I know what may be done. Go to the courtyard in the House of the Sun where the four fountains play, and sit you down among them. There you must sing to the fountains what is in your heart. If the fountains sing your song back to you, then you will know that a way will be found for you to go to your young man and be with him forever."

When the bird ceased speaking, Chuqui-llantu awoke. Wrapping herself in her cloak, Chuqui-llantu stole through the House of the Sun and went into the courtyard of the four fountains. The fountains stood for the four provinces of the Inca Empire, and each Daughter of the Sun bathed in the fountain that was named for her home province. Chuqui-llantu seated herself among the fountains and began to sing of her love for Acoya-napa and her longing for him, terrified all the while that she would be found and punished. As she sang, she listened with all ears, hoping beyond hope that what the bird in her dream had said would be true. And sure enough, after she had sung her song once, twice, thrice, the fountains began to sing back to her, singing the song of her love for the llama-herder. Chuqui-llantu was comforted, and she rejoiced that soon she would be able to love Acoya-napa in earnest, if she could but discover whether he felt the same about her.

Acoya-napa, for his part, had been struck by the beauty and grace of Chuqui-llantu, by her courtesy of speech and dignity of bearing, and on his way home with his flock, he could think of nothing else. But his heart was also pierced with sorrow for he knew that the Daughters of the Sun must spend their days in service to the great Inti, never marrying any man, least of all a lowly llama-herder who spent his days playing his panpipes on the mountainside.

When Acoya-napa got home, he went straight to his chamber and lay upon his bed, playing the most sorrowful tunes he could think of. His mother heard this and went in to see what was wrong. There she found her son, tears streaming down his face, playing laments on his panpipes.

"O my son, what is it that ails you?" she said.

"Today I met the most beautiful woman," said Acoya-napa, "and I love her with all my heart."

"Surely that is cause for rejoicing, not sadness," said his mother.

"Alas, no," said Acoya-napa, "for the one I love is a Daughter of the Sun, and she may never marry any man, least of all a lowly llama-herder such as I."

Now, Acoya-napa's mother was a very wise women, learned in all manner of remedies and cures. She said to him, "Take good heart, my son, for I am sure there is a remedy for your sorrow."

Leaving her son in his chamber, the woman went out upon the mountainside to collect herbs that she knew to be a cure for lovesickness and grief. When she returned to the house, she saw Chuqui-llantu and her companion coming toward her.

"Greetings, Mother," said Chuqui-llantu. "My companion and I have walked very far today. Would you have something that we might eat to refresh ourselves?"

"Certainly," said the old woman, and soon she had cooked a dish using the herbs she had culled on the mountainside.

Now, before setting out that day, Chuqui-llantu had learned where it was that Acoya-napa lived and which house was his, so she had not come to the place by chance. As she ate, she gazed about the house wondering where she might find Acoya-napa, but she did not see him for his mother had hidden him under a magic cloak that had once belonged to the beloved of the god Pachacamac himself. And the magic of the cloak was this: anyone or anything hidden underneath it would enter into the cloak and become one with it. Thus had Acoya-napa's mother hidden him, for when Chuqui-llantu looked about the house for her beloved, all she saw were the household things and in one room the beautiful cloak lying upon the bed.

"Oh!" cried Chuqui-llantu. "What a beautiful cloak! I do so wish I had something like it."

"You may have it," said the mother, "with a good will."

Chuqui-llantu took the cloak and arranged it about her shoulders, and with many thanks, she and her companion took their leave of

Acoya-napa's mother and returned to the House of the Sun. Those who dwelled in that sacred House took their evening meal together and then retired to their chambers for the night. Chuqui-llantu took the cloak and folded it tenderly at the foot of her bed and then wept for love until she was fast asleep.

Late that night, Chuqui-llantu was roused by someone softly calling her name. She woke and was startled to see Acoya-napa kneeling at her bedside, weeping many tears.

"O my beloved," said the young woman, "how do you come to be here?"

"When my mother put me under the cloak," said the llama-herder, "I became one with it, and you carried me into the House of the Sun on your own body. But in your presence, I resumed my own form once again, and the cloak became merely a piece of beautiful cloth."

Then the young people embraced one another very tenderly, and they spent the night in Chuqui-llantu's bed, delighting in one another.

In the morning, Acoya-napa covered himself with the cloak and once again became one with it. Pretending that she was going out for a walk as usual, Chuqui-llantu covered herself with the cloak and went out upon the mountainside. When she came to a place she deemed safe, she removed the cloak, and Acoya-napa recovered his own form. But alas, one of the guards from the House of the Sun suspected something was amiss and had followed Chuqui-llantu. He saw Acoya-napa come out of the cloak and take hands with Chuqui-llantu, and he raised the alarm.

Acoya-napa and Chuqui-llantu fled into the mountains, near a town called Calca. Soon they had outrun the guards, but they were very tired from their flight. Acoya-napa and Chuqui-llantu found a place to rest, and soon they were asleep in one another's arms. They had not slept long when a noise awakened them. The young people began to take flight once more, but they did not go many steps before they were both turned into stone.

There the two lovers stand to this day, in a place between Calca and Huayllabamba. And near that place also is a mountain with twin peaks, which is called Pitu-siray, which means "The Couple."

## The Legend of Lake Titicaca

*Lake Titicaca plays an important role in many Inca creation myths, but here we have the story of how the lake itself came to be, in a flood that was sent as retribution against a proud people who refused to honor the gods. Like many origin legends, the story of Lake Titicaca may contain grains of truth: in 2000, an archaeological expedition found the remains of an ancient temple and other civic structures under the lake, which probably were built by the Tiahuanaco people between 1,000 and 1,500 years ago. The Tiahuanaco people lived on the shores of Lake Titicaca and eventually were absorbed into the Inca Empire. It is possible that this legend is an imaginative just-so story that explains both the presence of the lake and the demise of the people who lived there in pre-Inca times.*

Once, long ago, high in the mountains, there was a wide, flat plain. And on this plain was a magnificent city. The buildings were made of the finest timber and stone and were trimmed with gold and silver. The people who lived there were proud and wealthy. They ate the finest food and dressed in the finest clothing. Their lives were good and easy, and they thought that they had the best city in the whole world. In fact, they often boasted of this to one another, and they did so so often that soon they began to think that they were not only the best city but that they were the lords of all creation. Their chief even began to think himself a god.

One day, a group of ragged beggars came to the city. They went through the streets crying out warnings. "The gods have seen your pride and arrogance, and they are displeased! Turn back from your evil ways, or you will be destroyed!"

The people of the city did not listen to the beggars. They laughed and mocked them, saying, "Who are you to tell us what to do? We are wealthy and strong while you are dressed in tattered clothing and have dirty faces. Go back where you came from!"

But the beggars did not stop making their warnings, even when the city people threw rotten vegetables at their heads.

After a few days, the beggars' warnings changed. "You have not listened to our warnings," they said, "so the gods have told us to tell you that you must leave your city. You must go away into the wilderness. You must climb up the mountains and repent of your evil ways, or the gods will destroy you and your city forever!"

The people of the city only laughed harder at this, and they only became more cruel toward the beggars. But the priests in the city temple came together to take counsel over what the beggars had been saying. "Maybe they are right," said one priest. "Maybe we should listen to them."

"Yes," said another. "I think it would be wise to do as they say."

And so, the priests agreed that they would listen to the beggars. They packed the things they would need for the journey, and they went out into the wilderness. They climbed up the mountains and prayed to the gods to be forgiven.

Now, after the priests had left the city, the people neglected the worship of the gods entirely. "If the priests won't stay to help us worship, then maybe there isn't anyone there to hear our prayers anyway. Maybe we are gods ourselves. And if we are gods, we have nothing to fear from these wretched beggars. Let us drive them from our city!"

But when they went to gather up the beggars and cast them outside the walls, they found that the beggars had already gone.

A few more days passed, and the city people said to themselves, "At last we have peace! No more beggars going about shouting at us! We can enjoy ourselves again." And so, they went back to their arrogant, wicked ways.

The next day dawned bright and sunny. But by afternoon, black clouds were gathering on the horizon. The people of the city paid this no mind for the clouds merely looked like rain clouds. Then other clouds began to appear, red clouds the color of blood. "What is this?" said the people. "We have never seen such clouds before. I wonder what it means?"

The black clouds and the red clouds advanced until the sky was covered in them, yet no rain fell. Night came, but there was no darkness because of the glowing redness of the clouds. A great sound of thunder rent the air. The ground shook. It shook and shook and did not stop shaking. Cracks appeared in the walls of the buildings, and soon the houses and shops and temples were falling down.

Rain began to fall from the sky, crimson rain the color of blood. The rivers near the city overflowed their banks. The waters flooded into the city. The people ran into the streets, screaming in terror, but there was nowhere for them to go. They could not escape the flood waters which rushed into the city, drowning the buildings and all the people. The rain fell, and the rivers overflowed until even the tops of the buildings were covered by deep water. And when the storm was over, a great lake stood where the city had once been. Of all the city people, only the priests who had listened to the beggars and gone to the mountains remained alive.

And that is how Lake Titicaca came to be on the great plain in the mountains.

# The Tale of Ollantay

*Apu Ollantay is a play in the Quechua language set during the ancient Inca Empire. The oldest copy of the play, which dates to about 1770, belonged to Antonio Valdés, who was a priest in Sicuani, Peru. Five other early manuscript copies survive today, with the first published editions dating from the middle of the nineteenth century. For a time, Valdés was believed to have been the author of the play, but now this has largely been discredited.*

*Scholars also debate the origins of the play. Because both the sources and many of the dramatic conventions of the play date from the eighteenth century, the actual genesis of the work is unclear. Some scholars have suggested that in the absence of sources earlier than the eighteenth century, we must consider* Apu Ollantay *to be an entirely colonial product, while others have argued that it is an old Inca tale that received dramatic treatment in colonial times. It is presented here as a prose tale with some omissions from the original play.*

*The name "Ollantay" also refers to the ancient stone fortress of Ollantay-tampu north of Cuzco. The early twentieth-century scholar Sir Clements Markham, who thought that the play was based on an ancient Inca legend, assumed that the fortress had been named after the protagonist of the drama.*

In the time of the Inca Pachacuti, there was a young warrior named Ollantay. Ollantay was strong and handsome and the most valiant fighter the Inca people had ever seen. Ollantay also was wise, and because of all his good qualities, the Inca Pachacuti trusted him and thought him one of his most valuable advisers and generals.

As a member of Pachacuti's court, Ollantay was often about the royal palace, and so he came to know Pachacuti's daughter, Cusi Coyllur, which means "Joyful Star." It was not long before the two young people fell very much in love with one another for Cusi Coyllur was beautiful and gracious just as Ollantay was brave and strong. Their love should have made them happy, but alas it caused them only pain, for brave and trusted as he was, Ollantay was but a commoner, and none but a man of noble blood might think to wed the daughter of the Inca.

For a long time, Cusi Coyllur and Ollantay contented themselves with brief meetings when they were able to find a few moments to be alone or fleeting glances across the room when they were in company, but finally, they could bear it no longer. They married one another in secret, and for a time, they were very happy, even though they still could not reveal their love to anyone else.

This time did not last, however. One day, Cusi Coyllur came to Ollantay and said, "We should not have to hide like this. We are man and wife, and we love one another. Let us go to my father and plead our case and ask to be formally married."

Ollantay agreed, although his heart warned him that it would be a fool's errand: the laws of the Incas were very strict, and Inca Pachacuti had been relentless in enforcing them. It seemed unlikely that the old man would set aside the traditional ways, even for his own daughter.

And so Cusi Coyllur and Ollantay begged audience of the Inca. They went before him and explained that they loved one another and that they wanted to be wed. But the Inca would have none of it. "Do you not know what it is you do?" he shouted. "No commoner may wed a daughter of the royal house. She is kin to the gods themselves, and you are but a mortal man and a servant. How dare you!"

Then Inca Pachacuti had his daughter taken to the House of the Sun where she was made one of the Daughters of the Sun, who are the women who serve in the temple and who are forbidden from ever marrying any man. Ollantay was told to go to his quarters and remain there, for the Inca was so wroth with him that he could not immediately think of a punishment sufficiently fitting for Ollantay's crime.

Ollantay chafed under his confinement and fretted about his wife. He knew that whatever punishment the Inca devised for him, the one end to it all would be his death. So, one night he escaped from his quarters. He went to his army captains and told them that he would be leaving. "The Inca Pachacuti has turned against me. I have lost everything I ever loved. I commend to you my good soldiers. Care for them well as you have seen me care for them. For myself, I will go far away into the mountains, and live there solitary. There is no longer any reason for me to stay here."

The captains protested at this. "You must not go! But if you cannot be swayed, then we will leave the service of the Inca and go with you, for you alone are our general, and we will serve none other."

"My friends," said Ollantay, "your love and loyalty do you credit. But I cannot ask you to come with me, for if you do, you will be deemed traitors, and the penalty for that is death. I have nothing to lose, for the Inca will take my life no matter what I do, but you have a choice in the matter."

The captains would not be swayed. They swore to accompany Ollantay and cast their lots in with his, whatever might come. And so it was that with a band of doughty men Ollantay made his way out of the capital and into the mountains.

Cusi Coyllur, meanwhile, was treated well by the Daughters of the Sun and their servants. She fell in with their ways and did her best to perform the duties expected of her. However, it soon became clear that she was with child, and when her time came, she was delivered of a daughter, whom she named Yma Sumac, which means "Most Beautiful." But because the Daughters of the Sun were forbidden to marry or have children, Yma Sumac was taken from her mother and raised as a foundling in another part of the temple.

Word came to the Inca that Ollantay had escaped his confinement and disappeared, along with a number of officers and soldiers from the army. Inca Pachacuti called to him Rumi-ñaui, his most trusted general. "Find them at once," roared the Inca, "and bring them to me that I may mete out justice to them! And take Cusi Coyllur and throw her in chains. This perfidy and the threat to my throne is all her doing."

"I will do as the Inca commands," said Rumi-ñaui. He conveyed the Inca's command to the servants of the House of the Sun, and Cusi Coyllur was imprisoned. Then Rumi-ñaui departed the court to begin his search for Ollantay.

Meanwhile, Ollantay had taken refuge with his men at the fortress of Ollantay-tampu, and there they gathered about them a mighty army. Ollantay had sent his servant back to Cuzco to see what response his flight had engendered with the Inca and to see what news might be had of Cusi Coyllur. Soon enough, the servant returned. "O Ollantay, the Inca is most wroth with you. He has set Rumi-ñaui the task of finding you and returning you to Cuzco, and a thousand men are at his command, searching throughout the empire."

"And of my beloved?" said Ollantay. "What news have you of her?"

"Alas, I could find no trace of her," said the servant. "Both she and the queen seem to have disappeared, and I fear the worst."

Hearing this, Ollantay despaired. Nothing now was holding him back from open rebellion. He rallied his army and the people of the region and spoke to them about the slights they had received at the hands of the Inca and of his own heart's sorrow for the loss of Cusi Coyllur. The people listened well to Ollantay's speech, and when he was finished, they raised up a great shout: "Long live Ollantay! Let Ollantay take the fringe! We will have none other as our Inca!"

When the Inca Pachacuti heard that Ollantay had taken up arms in rebellion, he recalled Rumi-ñaui and the thousand men from their search and commanded them to put his own army in order that they might defend the empire from the rebels. Quickly Rumi-ñaui marshalled his troops, and they headed into the mountains where they encountered Ollantay's army, and battle was joined. Both sides fought fiercely, but in the end, the army of the Inca was defeated, and Rumi-ñaui was forced to flee back to Cuzco, weakened and bleeding from many wounds, while Ollantay and his men returned to their fortress.

Ten years passed, and still Ollantay neither was defeated nor attempted to take Cuzco for his own. Ten years passed, and Yma Sumac, the baby born to Cusi Coyllur and daughter of Ollantay, grew into a strong young girl in the House of the Sun. Yma Sumac began to wonder why it was that others might come and go freely from the House of the Sun while she herself was forced to remain within its walls.

One night, Yma Sumac was unable to sleep, and so she went to take a walk in the courtyard of the House of the Sun. The entire household was asleep. The winds were calm, and the moon and stars bright in the sky. As Yma Sumac gazed at the night sky, a faint wailing came to her ears. "Surely that is the wind in the trees," thought Yma Sumac, but then she noted that there was no wind. Again, the wail arose, louder this time and followed by words. A woman's voice it was, praying to the Sun.

"O Sun," said the voice, "free me from these chains. I have done no evil. You who see all, take pity on me."

Yma Sumac knew not from where the voice came. She looked in many places but could find neither who it was that was in chains nor where they were held. Puzzled over the mystery and haunted by the wailing voice, she returned to her chamber and an uneasy slumber.

The next day, Yma Sumac sat in one of the gardens of the House of the Sun with a friend, who was a novice preparing to become a Daughter of the Sun. Both girls rose when they saw the Mother of the House approaching. The Mother addressed Yma Sumac, saying, "The time of choosing is upon you. Will you leave the outside world behind you and become a Daughter of the Sun? Or will you leave us?"

"How can I leave behind that which I have never seen?" said Yma Sumac. "Nevertheless, I have made my choice: I will not take the vows. I do not wish to become a Daughter of the Sun. I wish to leave this place as soon as I am able."

The Mother's face darkened for she had hoped to persuade the girl to stay within the House, under her control. "Very well," said the Mother and then turned and left the garden.

Yma Sumac and her friend stood watching the Mother leave. "Spiteful old tabby," muttered the young girl at the Mother's retreating back. Then she turned to Yma Sumac. "You're lucky," she said. "They won't be able to keep you here, and you have no family on the outside to tell you what to do or where to go. But I'll have to stay. My family wouldn't have me back for any money; they'd be too afraid of the Mother and the Priests of the House. I'll be a prisoner, just like that poor woman."

Yma Sumac looked sharply at her friend. "What woman?" she asked, trying to feign only little interest.

"You know, the one they keep in chains. The one who always wails at night. Surely you must have heard her. I have to bring her bread and water every day."

"Will you take me to her?" asked Yma Sumac. "I didn't know they kept prisoners here. I'd like to see the poor thing. Maybe I could bring her comfort."

"Very well," said the friend, "but it will have to be in secret. I'm not supposed to tell anyone else about her."

The friend told Yma Sumac how to get to the prisoner's cell and where she might hide until such time as the friend arrived with food and water for the prisoner. They agreed to meet there that very evening.

At the appointed time, the friend arrived and let Yma Sumac slip into the cell with her. Against one wall lay the form of a woman, dressed in rags and with unkempt hair, her leg in a manacle that was chained to the stone wall. The friend put the bread and water down next to the woman, who looked up wearily.

"I brought someone to see you," said the girl.

"Ah, a new face!" said the woman. "Ten long years have I been here, and only my jailers for company. And scant company at that."

Yma Sumac and the woman regarded one another for a moment. Then the girl spoke. "Why are you here?" she said. "What wrong have you done that they keep you here chained to that wall?"

"No wrong save to have loved the wrong man," said the woman. "I loved him against the wishes of my father and bore my beloved a child, but because I had done so without my father's blessing, the child was taken, and I was placed here, to live the rest of my days in sad misery."

"Oh," said Yma Sumac, "I also have been placed here, for I know neither my mother nor my father, and although I am not chained, yet I am a prisoner, for the Mother and the Priests will not let me leave this House even though I have no wish to become a Daughter of the Sun."

When the woman heard Yma Sumac's tale, she sat up a little straighter and looked long at the girl. "Tell me, if you will, what is your name and your age?"

"I am Yma Sumac, and I am ten years old," the girl replied.

The woman let out a little cry, and then she began to weep with joy. "Come to my arms, child," she said, "for you are my child indeed. You are the babe that was wrenched from me as soon as you drew breath. I am your mother, Cusi Coyllur, daughter of the Inca Pachacuti, and your father is the valiant Ollantay."

Then Cusi Coyllur and Yma Sumac embraced, and they wept many happy tears until finally Yma Sumac's friend reminded them that they could not linger, or Yma Sumac might be found where she had not leave to be and so come to grief at the hands of the Mother and the Priests of the House.

"Never fear, Mother," said Yma Sumac to Cusi Coyllur, "I shall find some way to free you. Give me but a space of a few days to find help, so that once again you may be free."

Then the girls took leave of Cusi Coyllur, and went back to their duties, promising one another not to reveal anything that had transpired in the prison cell.

Not long after Yma Sumac was reunited with her mother, the Inca Pachacuti died, and his son, Tupac Yupanqui, was chosen to succeed him. In a grand ceremony at the House of the Sun, Tupac Yupanqui assumed the imperial fringe and was proclaimed Inca by the Priests and all the nobles of the empire. During the celebration, the High Priest of the Sun prophesied that the rebels would return to allegiance with the Inca.

Among those attending the ceremony was the soldier Rumi-ñaui, who had lived in disgrace ever since his defeat at Ollantay-tambo. Thinking that he might regain some of his lost status with the new Inca by being the one to see the prophecy fulfilled, he begged an audience of Tupac Yupanqui and was admitted into the imperial presence.

"O my Inca, Child of the Sun and ruler of us all, I beg of you a boon," said Rumi-ñaui.

"Speak on," said the Inca.

"I have a plan, a ruse, that surely will deliver Ollantay into your hands and bring his rebels back under your control, as the High Priest said must happen. I ask only leave to do this thing for your greater glory and the safety of the empire."

"You have our leave so to do, but no blood must you shed" said the Inca, and Rumi-ñaui set out immediately to put his plan into effect. First, he readied his army and marched them to a place near Ollantay-tambo where they could lay hidden from the rebels. Then he donned ragged clothes that made him look like a beggar, disheveled his hair, and slashed bloody wounds into his own face. Thus disguised, he went to Ollantay-tambo, where he cried mercy of the rebels.

"Let me in, O let me in," he wailed in front of the gates. "Have mercy, for the gentle Pachacuti has passed, and his son, Tupac Yupanqui, rules us with great harshness."

The guard at the gate did not open directly but first sent for Ollantay. When Ollantay heard the supposed beggar's tale, he bade the gates be opened, for he did not recognize his old foe. Ollantay told his men to give the ragged man fresh clothing and food and medicine for his wounds. Then Ollantay said to his comrades, "Tonight we feast, for our great enemy, the Inca Pachacuti, is dead!"

And so, the rebels feasted, drinking and dancing until well into the night. When they ceased their feasting, besotted with drink, Rumi-ñaui opened the door of the stronghold to his own men, who slipped inside noiselessly and strangled many of the rebels in their sleep, thus keeping the Inca's command that no blood must be shed while reducing the number of rebels. Ollantay and his generals they took captive back to Cuzco.

Blindfolded and in bonds, Ollantay and the generals were brought before the Inca and his counsellors.

"Behold, O Mighty Inca," said Rumi-ñaui. "I bring before you the rebel Ollantay and the other conspirators against your empire and your throne. What judgement should be brought upon them for their treason?"

The Inca looked first to his High Priest, who said, "O Mighty Inca, I beg mercy on these men. Truly they have rebelled against the empire and the throne of the Inca, but they are doughty and resourceful. If you could win their allegiance, they would be useful allies."

Then the Inca looked to Rumi-ñaui, who said, "O Mighty Inca, I say that no mercy ought to be used. Rebels and traitors, they are, and remain a threat to your realm. Put them to death at once!"

"So shall it be," said the Inca. "We shall take them to a high place and have them thrown down to their deaths. Let us depart at once."

Ollantay and the generals were taken to a high place near Cuzco. They could feel and hear the wind swirling about them, and they knew that soon they would meet their fate. They were herded to the edge of the precipice and prepared themselves to be cast over, but instead of finding themselves falling, the blindfolds were taken from their eyes and they found themselves facing the Inca Tupac Yupanqui. They fell on their knees before him, and he said, "See now what mercy we use toward our enemies. We declare you not only to be free men but raised in station. Ollantay shall be a general of our armies and our chief deputy in Cuzco, and these others are to receive preferments as well, although lesser than those of Ollantay."

Hearing the merciful words of the Inca, the men bowed before him in gratitude and promised to him their everlasting loyalty. Rumiñaui, for his part, was shamed by the generosity of the Inca. He left Cuzco that very day and was never seen nor heard from again.

When they returned to Cuzco, Ollantay begged an audience of the Inca. "O Mighty Inca," he said, "you have been generous beyond measure to me. Let me show my loyalty and steadfastness by leading your armies into battle. We shall conquer many peoples and thus increase your realm and your store of treasure."

"That is a generous offer, O my deputy," said the Inca, "but such deeds shall I only call for when they are needed, and today is not that day. Take you a wife, and live quietly and serve me here in Cuzco."

"Alas," said Ollantay, "never shall I marry, for once I had a wife, and we had but a few days together before she was taken from me. Ever have I lived in sorrow since, and I will have no other wife for the rest of my days."

As Ollantay finished speaking, the door of the audience chamber swung open, and a young girl rushed in and prostrated herself before the Inca. A servant ran in close behind and bowed low, saying, "A thousand pardons, O Mighty Inca, but this young one from the House of the Sun evaded me, and before I could stop her, she came in here. I ask your mercy on us both for this disturbance."

"Never fear," said the Inca, "We will not have it said that we do not listen even to the youngest of our subjects. What is it you need of us, little one?"

"O Mighty Inca," said the girl, "my name is Yma Sumac, and all my days I have lived as a foundling in the House of the Sun. Lately I have learned who my parents are. My mother is cruelly held in a prison cell where she languishes and must die soon if she does not receive your mercy. I swear to you and to your Father the Sun that my mother has done no wrong. I beg you to come see for yourself how she has been treated, that you might be moved to pity and release her."

"We will not have it said that we hold prisoners who are guiltless," said the Inca. "Show us where your mother is kept, and we will make judgement proper to the situation. Our deputy also will accompany us in this."

Now, Yma Sumac had never seen her father, and even though he was present in the audience chamber, the Inca had never pronounced his name. Nor had Ollantay ever seen his child; and thus it was that neither recognized the other, and so as strangers they went together with the Inca on his mission of mercy.

When they arrived at the House of the Sun, the Inca commanded the Mother of the House to appear before him and to show him where the prisoner was kept. Together they went to the prison cell. The Mother of the House opened it, and all beheld the wasted form of Cusi Coyllur.

"Release her from her bonds, and have her stand before us," said the Inca.

This was done, and soon Cusi Coyllur was standing, trembling in her rags, with her head bowed before Tupac Yupanqui and his companions, her long, unkempt hair covering her face. The Inca instantly took pity on her and was wroth with the Mother of the House. "You have used this woman very ill," he said. "Even though she were your prisoner, still you had a duty to keep her well. This you did not do, and so we release you from your office. Another shall have the station of Mother of the House."

The Mother could do no other than bow to the Inca and depart. Once she was gone, the Inca said to Cusi Coyllur, "Tell me, if you can, who you are and why you have been imprisoned here?"

"O Mighty Inca," said Cusi Coyllur, "I beg of you your mercy. My name is Cusi Coyllur, daughter of the Inca Pachacuti. I was imprisoned here by my father's order for I loved the valiant Ollantay against his wishes and bore of him a child, the very one who has brought you to this place. As soon as the child drew breath, she was taken from me and I was chained here, to spend my days in misery, although my crime was nothing other than love."

The Inca and Ollantay stood thunderstruck at what the woman had said. So wretched was her state that the Inca had not recognized his sister, nor had Ollantay known her as his very own beloved wife.

"Is this true?" said the Inca.

"It is," said Cusi Coyllur. "I swear by the imperial fringe you wear and by the Sun Himself that I tell no lie."

"Look at us, and let us see your face," said the Inca.

Cusi Coyllur lifted her head and brushed her hair aside. Although she was thin and wan, Ollantay and the Inca both knew her, and both cried out with joy and pity.

"Bring fresh robes for this woman," commanded the Inca, "and bear her in state back to our own dwelling. Give her a chamber and all refreshment, for she is our noble sister and the wife of our trusted deputy."

Ollantay went to Cusi Coyllur and embraced her tenderly. "I had not thought to see you again," he said, "and it pains me that you have been so ill used. But perhaps now the Inca will pardon you for having married a commoner, and we will be able to live together in peace."

"A commoner you may have been when you were wed," said the Inca, "but a nobleman shall you be as of this moment. We raise you in station and wish you long life and much joy with the wife of your heart, whom we also love, for she is our sister, and with your dear daughter, for she is our niece."

Yma Sumac had been standing aside, watching all of this in silence, for she was overcome with joy and gratitude for the mercy of the Inca and also with the knowledge that the man who had accompanied her and their lord to the prison cell was none other than her own father.

Ollantay turned to Yma Sumac. "Come here, child. Let me look on you, for I am your father and am grateful for your courage and steadfast love of your mother."

Then Ollantay embraced his daughter, and the family, now reunited after ten long and bitter years, shed many tears of joy.

True to his word, the Inca gave a pleasant dwelling to his sister and her family within the palace. He saw that they never wanted for the least thing, and there Ollantay, Cusi Coyllur, and Yma Sumac lived for the rest of their days, in peace and harmony.

# Here's another book that I think you'd be interested in:

And another one…

# Bibliography

Bellos, Alex. "Ancient Wonder: Pre-Inca Ruins Found in Lake Titicaca." *The Guardian*, 23 August 2000. <https://www.theguardian.com/world/2000/aug/24/bolivia>, accessed 11 January 2019.

Betanzos, Juan de. *Narrative of the Incas.* Trans. and ed. Roland Hamilton and Dana Buchanan. Austin: University of Texas Press, 1996.

Bierhorst, John, ed. *Latin American Folktales: Stories from Hispanic and Indian Traditions*. New York: Pantheon Books, 2002.

———. *The Mythology of South America*. New York: William Morrow and Company, Inc., 1988.

———, ed. and trans. *Black Rainbow: Legends of the Incas and Myths of Ancient Peru*. New York: Farrar, Straus & Giroux, 1976.

Brinton, Daniel G. *American Hero-Myths: A Study in the Native Religions of the Western Continent.* Philadelphia: H. C. Watts & Co., 1882.

Carpenter, Frances. *South American Wonder Tales*. Chicago: Follett Publishing Company, 1969.

Cobo, Bernabe. *Inca Religion and Customs*. Trans. and ed. Roland Hamilton. Austin: University of Texas Press, 1990.

———. *History of the Inca Empire*. Trans. and ed. Roland Hamilton. Austin: University of Texas Press, 1979.

Colum, Padraic. *Orpheus: Myths of the World*. New York: Macmillan, 1930.

Cossins, Daniel. "We Thought the Incas Couldn't Write. These Knots Change Everything." *The New Scientist*, 26 September 2018. <https://www.newscientist.com/article/mg23931972-600-we-thought-the-incas-couldnt-write-these-knots-change-everything/>, accessed 26 November 2018.

Dixon-Kennedy, Mike. *Native American Myth & Legend: An A-Z of People and Places*. London: Blandford, 1996.

Elliot, L. E. "Ollantay: An Ancient Inca Drama." *The Pan-American Magazine* 33/1 (1921): 281-290.

Gifford, Douglas. *Warriors, Gods and Spirits from Central and South American Mythology*. New York: Peter Bedrick Books, 1983.

Hills, Elijah Clarence. *The Quechua Drama* Ollanta. *Romanic Review* 5/2 (1914): 127-176.

Kuss, Daniele. *Myths and Legends of Incas*. New York: Marshall Cavendish, 1991.

La Barre, Weston. "The Aymara: History and Worldview." *The Journal of American Folklore* 79/311 (1966): 130-144.

Markham, Clements R., ed. *The Incas of Peru*. New York: Dutton, 1910.

———, ed. *History of the Incas, by Pedro Sarmiento de Gamboa, and the Execution of the Inca Tupac Amaru, by Captain Baltasar de Ocampo.* Farnham: Ashgate Publishing Ltd., 2010.

———, ed. *Narratives of the Rites and Laws of the Yncas.* Farnham: Ashgate Publishing Ltd., 2010.

———, ed. *The Second Part of the Chronicle of Peru by Pedro de Cieza de Leon.* Farnham: Ashgate Publishing Ltd., 2010.

———, ed. *The Travels of Pedro de Cieza de Leon, A.D. 1532-50, Contained in the First Part of His Chronicle of Peru.* Volume I. Farnham: Ashgate Publishing Ltd., 2010.

Osborne, Harold. *South American Mythology.* Feltham: The Hamlyn Publishing Group, Ltd., 1968.

Pan-American Union. *Folk Songs and Stories of the Americas.* Washington, DC: Organization of American States, 1971.

Roberts, Timothy R. *Myths of the World: Gods of the Maya, Aztecs, and Incas.* New York: Friedman/Fairfax Publishers, 1996.

Salomon, Frank, and George L. Urioste, trans. *The Huarochirí Manuscript: A Testament of Ancient and Colonial Andean Religion.* Austin: University of Texas Press, 1991.

Schmitt, Martha. *World Myths and Legends II: South America.* Belmont: Fearon/James/Quercus, 1993.

Steele, Paul R., with Catherine J. Allen. *Handbook of Inca Mythology.* Santa Barbara: ABC-CLIO, Inc., 2004.

Suarez-Rivas, Maite, ed. *Latino Read-Aloud Stories.* New York: Black Dog & Leventhal Publishers, 2000.

Urton, Gary. *Inca Myths*. Austin: University of Texas Press, 1999.

Vega, Garcilasso de. *First Part of the Royal Commentaries of the Yncas*. Trans. Clement R. Markham. 2 vols. London: Hakluyt Society, 1869-71.

Witherspoon, Anna. *Let's See South America*. Dallas: The Southern Publishing Company, 1939.

www.ingramcontent.com/pod-product-compliance
Lightning Source LLC
Chambersburg PA
CBHW070049230426
43661CB00005B/826